Clinics in Developmental Medicine No. 76

The Floppy Infant

2nd Edition

By

VICTOR DUBOWITZ

1980

Spastics International Medical Publications

LONDON: William Heinemann Medical Books Ltd.

PHILADELPHIA: J. B. Lippincott Co.

ISBN 0433 07902 9

Printed in England at THE LAVENHAM PRESS LTD., Lavenham, Suffolk

Contents

	FOREWORD	vii
Chapter 1	INTRODUCTION AND REVIEW OF THE LITERATURE	1
	The Floppy Infant Syndrome	1
	Historical Survey	1
	Infantile Progressive Spinal Muscular Atrophy	2
	Amyotonia Congenita	2
	Congenital Myopathy	3
	Essential Hypotonia	3
	Symptomatic Hypotonia	3
	Benign Congenital Hypotonia	3
	Non-progressive Congenital Myopathies	6
Chapter 2	A PRACTICAL APPROACH TO THE DIAGNOSIS AND CLASSIFICATION OF THE FLOPPY INFANT	10
	Assessment of Hypotonia	10
	Differential Diagnosis and Classification	11
PART I	PARALYTIC DISORDERS: MUSCULAR WEAKNESS WITH INCIDENTAL HYPOTONIA. NEUROMUSCULAR DISORDERS	19
Chapter 3	SPINAL MUSCULAR ATROPHIES	20
	Infantile Spinal Muscular Atrophy	20
	Clinical Features	20
	Course and Prognosis	23
	Diagnosis	23
	Management	25
	Genetics	26
	Benign Variants	26
	Intermediate Severity Spinal Muscular Atrophy	26
	Onset	26
	Clinical Picture	27
	Course and Prognosis	29
	Deformities	29
	Diagnosis	30
	Management	30
	Genetics	31
Chapter 4	CONGENITAL MYOPATHIES	33
	Clinical Features	33
	Investigations	34
	A. 'Structural' Congenital Myopathies	35
	Central Core Disease	35
	Minicore Disease	38
	Nemaline Myopathy ('Rod Body' Myopathy)	38
	Myotubular Myopathy	41
	Myotubular Myopathy with Type 1 Fibre Hypotrophy	43
	Severe X-linked Myotubular Myopathy	44
	Mixed Myopathies	47
	Co-existence of Nemaline Myopathy and Cores in Same Patient	47
	Co-existence of Minicores with Whorled Fibres	48

Congenital Fibre Type Disproportion   50
Congenital Type 1 Fibre Predominance   54
Mitochondrial Myopathies   55
Mitochondrial-Lipid-Glycogen Storage Myopathy   56
Myopathies with Abnormalities of Other Subcellular Organelles   60
Non-specific Congenital Myopathies; 'Minimal Change' Myopathy   61
B. Metabolic Myopathies   63
Glycogenoses   63
   Type II Glycogenosis   63
   Type III Glycogenosis   67
   Type IV Glycogenosis   69
Abnormalities of Lipid Metabolism   69
   Carnitine Deficiency   69
   Carnitine Palmityl Transferase Deficiency   70
Periodic Paralysis   71

Chapter 5   OTHER NEUROMUSCULAR DISORDERS   72
Congenital Myotonic Dystrophy   72
   Clinical Features   72
   Clinical Course   75
   Diagnosis   76
   Management   76
   Genetic Counselling   77
   Antenatal Diagnosis   77
   Antenatal Treatment   77
Congenital Muscular Dystrophy   77
   Clinical Picture   82
   Investigations   84
   Genetics   85
   Management   85
Duchenne Muscular Dystrophy   86
Myasthenia   87
   Neonatal Myasthenia   87
   Congenital or Infantile Myasthenia   88
Botulism   89
Peripheral Neuropathies: (A) Acquired   89
   Poliomyelitis   89
   Polyneuropathy   90
Peripheral Neuropathies: (B) Hereditary   91
   Hypertrophic Neuropathy (peroneal muscular atrophy) (HMSN Type I)   91
   Hypertrophic Neuropathy of Infancy (HMSN Type III)   92
   Progressive Degenerative Disorders of the Central Nervous System   92
      Metachromatic Leucodystrophy   92
      Globoid Cell Leucodystrophy   92
      Neuraxonal Dystrophy   92
      Other Central Nervous System Disorders   93

PART II   NON-PARALYTIC DISORDERS: HYPOTONIA WITHOUT SIGNIFICANT WEAKNESS   95

Chapter 6   DISORDERS OF THE CENTRAL NERVOUS SYSTEM   96
Non-specific Mental Deficiency   96
Hypotonic Cerebral Palsy   99
Birth Trauma, Haemorrhage, Hypoxia   100
   Perinatal Drug Influences   100

Chromosomal Disorders: Down's Syndrome (Mongolism, Trisomy 21) 103
Metabolic Disorders 105
  Abnormalities of Amino Acid Metabolism 105
    Hyperlysinaemia 105
    Non-ketotic Hyperglycinaemia 106
  Organic Acidaemias/Organic Acidurias 107
  Miscellaneous Rare Metabolic Disorders with Marked Hypotonia 109
    Infantile Type of Neuronal Ceroid Lipofuscinosis 109
    Mulibrey Nanism 110
    Muscle, Eye and Brain Disease 110
    Cerebro-hepato-renal Syndrome (Zellweger's disease) 111
    Oculo-cerebro-renal Syndrome (Lowe's syndrome) 111
  The Sphingolipidoses 111

Chapter 7   CONNECTIVE TISSUE DISORDERS 115
  Congenital Laxity of Ligaments 115
  Ehlers-Danlos Syndrome 116
  Marfan Syndrome 116
  Mucopolysaccharidoses 117

Chapter 8   MISCELLANEOUS 126
  Prader-Willi Syndrome (Hypotonia-obesity Syndrome) 126
  Metabolic, Nutritional and Endocrine Disorders 132
    Metabolic 132
    Nutritional 132
    Endocrine 133
  Congenital Heart Disease 133
  'Benign Congenital Hypotonia' ('Essential Hypotonia') 133

Chapter 9   DIAGNOSTIC PROCEDURES 139
  Associated Clinical Features 139
    Hypotonia with Associated Sucking/Swallowing Difficulty in the
      Newborn Period 139
    Hypotonia with Associated Facial Weakness 140
    Hypotonia with Associated External Ophthalmoplegia 140
    Hypotonia with 'Arthrogryposis' 140
  Electrodiagnosis 141
    Nerve Conduction Velocity 141
    Electromyography 142
  Serum Enzymes 143
  Muscle Biopsy 144

REFERENCES 147
INDEX 155

To the memory of

RONALD MAC KEITH.

1908-1977

Foreword

When I wrote the first edition of this floppy infant monograph I had two main objectives in mind. The first was to try to resolve the chaos in terminology which had crept into this whole field and to relegate to the oblivion they deserved such meaningless diagnostic labels as 'amyotonia congenita', 'universal muscular hypoplasia' and so forth, and also to put into proper perspective other descriptive terms such as 'essential hypotonia' and 'benign congenital hypotonia'. The second objective was to try to provide a practical clinical approach to the assessment and differential diagnosis of the floppy infant syndrome and to differentiate the neuromuscular causes from the non-neuromuscular causes. In addition, the application of histochemical techniques to the assessment of muscle biopsy from the early 1960s was beginning to reap the benefits of recognizing new and distinctive syndromes of muscle disorder, some of which were of importance in relation to the floppy infant syndrome.

The ensuing years have seen a consolidation and expansion of our knowledge in relation to these various neuromuscular disorders, and also marked advances in other disorders associated with hypotonia, for example the connective tissue disorders and various metabolic disorders such as the mucopolysaccharidoses and sphingolipidoses.

Although the chaos in terminology has now largely been resolved, I thought it would be of interest to retain much of the original introductory chapter in order to give the historical background and perspective to the evolution of the floppy infant syndrome. I have also retained the basic structure of the second chapter on the approach to the diagnosis and classification of the floppy infant.

The remaining sections of the book have been almost entirely rewritten and brought up to date and, in addition, much new clinical material has been included.

The section on diagnostic procedures has also been completely rewritten, and our cumulative experience with the application of electrodiagnostic techniques to the floppy infant, and also the application of needle biopsy as opposed to open biopsy as a diagnostic procedure, has been incorporated.

While trying to include a completely up-to-date review of all the exciting biochemical advances in our understanding of the sphingolipidoses, mucopolysaccharidoses and connective tissue disorders, I have also tried not to miss the wood for the trees in relation to these relatively rare disorders but to retain the basic emphasis of the monograph, which I would still like to be primarily a clinically oriented guide for the benefit of the clinician in practice.

Acknowledgments

I am very grateful to a large number of people for making this volume possible. Firstly the late Ronnie Mac Keith who was on my back for a number of years encouraging me to do a second edition; Valerie Chalk for her enthusiasm and expert secretarial help with many aspects of the book's gestation; Mr. Alan Tunstill in Sheffield and Mr. David Hawtin at Hammersmith for the excellent clinical photographs; Christine Hutson for technical help with the muscle biopsies and additional help in many other ways; Caroline Maunder-Sewry for the electron microscopy; Doig Simmonds and Antonia Lant for the art work in the various charts; the many paediatric colleagues who have continued to refer their interesting muscle patients; and finally Dr. Aidan Macfarlane and S.I.M.P. editorial staff, particularly Robert Torday and Bernard Hayes.

CHAPTER 1

Introduction and Review of the Literature

The clinician is often faced with the infant who is limp or immobile. Some of these children are paralysed, but others have no apparent abnormality in the neuromuscular system. In recent years such children have been collectively grouped under the title of 'the floppy infant syndrome'.

The purpose of this book is to discuss the recognition and diagnosis of the floppy infant syndrome, to review some of the more important causes, and to provide a practical approach to the assessment and management of these children.

The floppy infant syndrome

The floppy or hypotonic infant has been likened to a rag doll. This is a very apt comparison, since the rag doll mimics many of the clinical criteria for the diagnosis of the floppy infant syndrome.

There are three main clinical features which we associate with hypotonia:
(1) bizarre or unusual postures;
(2) diminished resistance of the joints to passive movement;
(3) increase in the range of movement of the joints.

In the newborn period, the floppy infant will usually present with paucity of active movements and with unusual postures; the older infant usually presents with delay in achievement of motor milestones.

Muscular hypotonia is a common symptom in infancy. It may be associated with a wide variety of apparently unrelated conditions. It may be the presenting feature of a neuromuscular disorder; it may occur in mentally retarded children or in the early phase of cerebral palsy; it may be a manifestation of a connective tissue disorder; it may be associated with various metabolic disorders in infancy; it may be an incidental and non-specific sign in any acutely ill child; it may be completely physiological in the premature infant; and it may occur as a completely isolated symptom in an otherwise normal child.

At the time of writing the first edition of this monograph, the subject had become a complex one, partly because of confusion in nomenclature and partly because of the exhaustive lists of potential causes that were a feature of most reviews. It was not my intention to list all the possible causes of hypotonia, neatly subdivided and tabulated on an anatomical or pathological basis. I wished, rather, to highlight some of the more common causes of infantile hypotonia, to present a practical approach to the clinical diagnosis of the floppy infant and to discuss some of the special techniques which may help in the diagnosis.

Historical survey

A number of neuromuscular disorders initially formed the nucleus of the floppy infant syndrome. As the list gradually increased in length, so it expanded in breadth. With this expansion came chaos in terminology (Table 1.I). This was partly due to the use of the same name for different entities, and partly due to the use of different names for the same condition. In addition, recent specialized techniques of investigation have shown that many conditions previously looked upon as specific entities are no more than clinical symptom complexes, which can be caused by different underlying muscular disorders. The following are the more important descriptions of disease entities, and contributions to the classification of the floppy infant.

Infantile progressive spinal muscular atrophy

In a series of papers, Werdnig (1891, 1894) and Hoffmann (1893, 1897, 1900) described in great detail the clinical and pathological features of familial infantile progressive spinal muscular atrophy (Werdnig-Hoffmann's disease). Werdnig's two cases were siblings, and the seven cases of Hoffmann came from four families. All the patients were apparently normal at birth and developed weakness of the trunk and limbs in the latter half of the first year of life. All died of respiratory infection at ages ranging from 14 months to 6 years and at autopsy there were degenerative changes in the anterior horn cells of the cord and in some of the motor nuclei of the cranial nerves.

Amyotonia congenita

In a rather poorly documented, brief paper, Oppenheim (1900) claimed to have seen a number of infants who were floppy at or soon after birth, but did not subsequently deteriorate as in the case of Werdnig-Hoffmann's disease. There was hypotonia, or even atonia, of the trunk and extremities, the tendon reflexes were

TABLE 1.I
Chaos in terminology

Terminology	Author
Infantile progressive spinal muscular atrophy	Werdnig (1891) Hoffmann (1893)
Myatonia congenita	Oppenheim (1900)
Amyotonia congenita	Collier and Wilson (1908)
Benign congenital myopathy	Batten (1903) Turner (1940)
Congenital universal muscular hypoplasia	Krabbe (1947)
Amyotonia congenita = Infantile muscular atrophy	Greenfield and Stern (1927)
Amyotonia congenita = Symptom complex	Brandt (1950)
Essential or primary hypotonia	Sobel (1926)
Essential hypotonia	Zellweger (1946)
Benign congenital hypotonia	Walton (1956)

diminished or absent, the joints had an increased range of passive movement and there was reduced spontaneous movement. He suggested the term *myatonia congenita* for this condition, which apparently was non-familial. He subsequently described in more detail two children, aged 19 months and 12 years respectively, who conformed to this pattern (Oppenheim 1904, 1912).

In order to avoid confusion in terminology between Oppenheim's myatonia congenita and *myotonia congenita* (Thomsen's disease), Collier and Wilson (1908) suggested it be called *amyotonia congenita*, a term which was widely adopted in the English literature. However, the term myatonia congenita was retained in much of the continental literature.

Controversy soon arose as to whether amyotonia congenita was indeed a separate disease entity. The early onset, as opposed to the cases of Werdnig-Hoffmann with their later onset, soon proved an unreliable criterion, and in 1902 Beevor had already described a familial case of infantile muscular atrophy with paralysis present at birth. Further confusion followed when Rothmann (1909) found at autopsy the typical features of spinal muscular atrophy in the spinal cord of a child from Oppenheim's clinic, who, in a separate report, was looked upon as a typical case of myatonia congenita (Habermann 1910).

Collier and Wilson (1908) reviewed in detail 21 cases of amyotonia congenita from the literature and a further four of their own. It is apparent from the case histories that some conform to the typical nature of infantile muscular atrophy and that others undoubtedly were examples of a more benign variant of infantile muscular atrophy. They also quote Oppenheim as follows: 'Professor Oppenheim tells us that though he has had several cases under his observation for years which have improved markedly, yet at present they are all far from complete recovery.'

Authors soon become rather indiscriminate in their terminology. Thus two papers appearing side by side in the same issue of the *American Journal of Diseases of Children* described cases with similar histological features and progressive courses, yet one was interpreted as amyotonia congenita with embryonic muscle (Holmes 1920) and the other as infantile muscular atrophy with denervation of the muscle (Huenekens and Bell 1920).

In 1927, Greenfield and Stern made a detailed study of the pathological changes in amyotonia congenita and infantile muscular atrophy. From a review of 25 cases of amyotonia congenita with autopsy reports in the literature and three cases of their own, they concluded that the pathological changes in the nervous system were identical with those in infantile muscular atrophy. It is apparent that the clinical diagnosis in most of these must have been incorrect, since amyotonia congenita should, by definition, be characterized by improvement and not death. Moreover, a number of cases were familial, and many had their onset after birth.

In a critical review of 297 cases of amyotonia congenita in the literature, Brandt (1950) found that 106 were infantile muscular atrophy or other affections not conforming to amyotonia congenita. Of the remaining 191 cases, clinical improvement occurred in only 86, and detailed analysis of these showed that in only 20 was the improvement well enough documented to exclude Werdnig-Hoffmann's disease. These 20 cases formed such a small and heterogeneous group that it seemed

TABLE 1.II

Causes of 'amyotonia congenita': Brandt (1950)

1. *Other progressive degenerative lesions in the neuromuscular system*
Atypical progressive muscular atrophy
Infantile amaurotic idiocy
Diffuse sclerosis of the brain
Hereditary amyotrophic lateral sclerosis
Hereditary ataxia
Dystrophia myotonica

2. *Congenital or very early acquired defects in the central nervous system due to developmental disturbances, haemorrhage or infection*
Congenital cerebellar ataxia
Atonic-astatic diplegia and spastic diplegia, with initial stage of hypotonia
Birth traumatic haemorrhages or circulatory disturbances in the central nervous system
Mental deficiency with symptomatic muscular hypotonia
Hydrocephalus
Syringomyelia — spina bifida

3. *Postnatal infections in the central nervous system or in the striated musculature*
Encephalitis, poliomyelitis, myelitis, polyneuritis,
myositis, dermatomyositis, polymyositis

4. *Tumours of the central nervous system*

5. *Constitutional affections accompanied by muscular flabbiness or articular laxity*
Mongoloid idiocy, congenital myxoedema, osteopsathyrosis,
arachnodactyly, constitutional hereditary looseness of joints,
Ehlers-Danlos syndrome, universal muscular hypoplasia

6. *Muscular flabbiness*
In rickets, digestive disorders, protracted generalised infection and Addison's disease

7. *Myasthenia Gravis*

TABLE 1.III

Causes of 'amyotonia congenita': Walton (1956)

Neuromuscular disorders	
Infantile spinal muscular atrophy	67
Benign congenital hypotonia with complete recovery	8
Benign congenital hypotonia with incomplete recovery	9
Congenital 'myopathy' with myasthenic features	1
Progressive muscular dystrophy	3
Polymyositis	1
Cerebral disorders	
'Cerebral palsy'	6
Mental defect	8
Nutritional and metabolic disorders	
Scurvy	2
Skeletal disorders	
Arachnodactyly	1
Multiple congenital defects	1
Congenital dislocation of hip	1
Other disorders	
Spinal ganglioneuroma	1

4

questionable whether they represented any neurological entity. Brandt concluded that Oppenheim's amyotonia congenita was not a specific entity but merely a diagnosis of a symptom complex.

Thus it was not surprising that contemporary clinicians continued to be confused, and frequently used the term amyotonia congenita for a case of infantile muscular atrophy, and not for a benign condition as originally designated by Oppenheim.

Congenital myopathy

To add further to the complexity of aetiology, Batten (1903) described three children with 'a myopathy of an infantile type'. Although Batten looked upon this as a separate disease entity, the clinical features of 'extreme flaccidity of the muscles, associated with an entire loss of the deep reflexes, most marked at the time of birth and always showing a tendency to slow and progressive amelioration', were very similar to Oppenheim's amyotonia congenita. This family was studied many years later by Turner (1940, 1949, 1962). In the course of time the hypotonia disappeared and atrophy of proximal muscles developed. In one patient no abnormality was found in the spinal cord at autopsy and the muscle still showed a myogenic rather than a neurogenic lesion.

Essential hypotonia

In 1926 Sobel described 45 children with generalized flabbiness but without muscular weakness and with normal tendon reflexes: most of them recovered. The joints showed marked hypermobility and Sobel thought there was abnormal laxity of the joint ligaments and capsule, in addition to the hypotonia. He looked upon this condition as 'essential or primary hypotonia'. In some cases a parent had also been hypotonic in infancy. Cases of 'joint hypotonia' with familial distribution had previously been recorded by Finkelstein (1916).

Symptomatic hypotonia

In a study of 131 hospital cases previously diagnosed as amyotonia congenita (Oppenheim), infantile progressive muscular atrophy (Werdnig-Hoffmann), progressive muscular dystrophy, or synonymous titles, Brandt (1950) revised the diagnoses to either infantile muscular atrophy or a number of other underlying conditions in all but 13 cases. Of the cases not due to infantile muscular atrophy, the broad classification into which Brandt suggested subdividing his cases, and similar cases in the literature, is shown in Table 1.II.

This was the first attempt at a systematic classification of hypotonic infants and Brandt stressed the fact that amyotonia congenita could no longer be looked upon as a single entity, but was a symptom complex. Further reviews of the causes of symptomatic hypotonia were given by Tizard (1954) and Sandifer (1955).

Benign congenital hypotonia

Walton (1956) reviewed the clinical course of 115 patients who had previously been diagnosed as amyotonia congenita at the National Hospital for Nervous Diseases, Queen Square, or the Hospital for Sick Children, Great Ormond Street, London, between the years 1930 and 1953. Of the 109 patients traced by letter, 56 had died, and 55 of these conformed to infantile muscular atrophy. The revised diagnoses in the 109 cases are listed in Table 1.III.

Walton used the term *benign congenital hypotonia* as a descriptive title for 17 patients with a similar clinical picture of initial hypotonia and a tendency to gradual improvement. Eight recovered completely but nine were left with residual weakness. Although the natural history of these cases resembled Oppenheim's original description of amyotonia congenita, Walton preferred the title *benign hypotonia* in view of 'the unfortunate connotations acquired by 'amyotonia congenita' since it was originally introduced'. He also saw a resemblance between his cases with incomplete recovery and the patients with 'benign congenital myopathy' of Batten (1903) and Turner (1940, 1949) and 'congenital universal muscular hypoplasia' of Krabbe (1947, 1958).

In a more detailed clinical report on these patients, Walton (1957*a*) noted that electromyography in two cases with complete recovery and in three with incomplete recovery showed a pattern suggestive of a myopathic disorder. However, muscle biopsy in two cases who recovered and in four with residual weakness showed no abnormality. Walton concluded that 'benign congenital hypotonia is a distinctive clinical syndrome, which may result from a congenital neuromuscular abnormality of varying severity. In certain cases the abnormality is mild and may be overcome in time by the process of post-natal development, while in others the defect is more severe and there is a residual disability which persists throughout life.' Walton (1957*b*) sub-divided and supplemented his previous classification of cases (Walton 1956), as shown in Table 1.IV.

Non-progressive congenital myopathies

The recognition of a number of *non-progressive congenital myopathies* with specific structural abnormalities, such as central core disease (Shy and Magee 1956), rod body or nemaline myopathy (Conen *et al.* 1963, Shy *et al.* 1963), myotubular

TABLE 1.IV
Classification of hypotonic infant: Walton (1957b)

A. *Infantile muscular atrophy and related syndromes*

B. *Symptomatic hypotonia:*
1. Neuromuscular and muscular disorders:
   progressive muscular dystrophy, myasthenia gravis, polymyositis, infantile polyneuritis
2. Cerebral disorders:
   'Cerebral palsy' (flaccid diplegia, congenital athetosis), cerebral birth injury, mental defect, kernicterus, cerebral lipidosis
3. Nutritional and metabolic disorders:
   rickets, scurvy, cretinism, malnutrition, coeliac disease, glycogen storage disease, chronic infection following acute illness
4. Skeletal disorders:
   osteogenesis imperfecta, arachnodactyly
5. Other disorders:
   congenital heart disease, other congenital abnormalities, spinal cord birth injury

C. *Benign congenital hypotonia*

---

myopathy (Spiro *et al.* 1966), and myopathies associated with abnormalities of the mitochondria (Shy *et al.* 1966) provided an explanation for at least some of the cases of so-called benign congenital hypotonia, particularly those with incomplete resolution. These congenital myopathies can present in early infancy with a floppy infant syndrome and delay in attaining motor milestones, or later with a non-progressive proximal (or more general) muscular weakness simulating muscular dystrophy.

Another group of cases contributing to a clinical picture of 'benign congenital hypotonia' with incomplete resolution could well be the more benign forms of spinal muscular atrophy in infancy (Byers and Banker 1961, Dubowitz 1964). Another condition with profound hypotonia at birth and gradual and complete resolution of the hypotonia is the Prader-Willi syndrome (Prader *et al.* 1956, Prader and Willi 1963). However, this is a complex syndrome in which severe hypotonia is only one of the features (see Chapter 8).

Meanwhile further extensive reviews were published, augmenting the differential diagnosis of hypotonia. Paine (1963) reviewed 133 children, aged between six months and 2½ years, referred because of slow motor development, and in whom hypotonia was an incidental feature at examination. The majority of cases of infantile muscular atrophy, which would have become evident at a younger age, were not included in the review. The largest group were the cerebral palsies, comprising 68 cases; 25 had mental or psychomotor retardation; seven spinal muscular atrophy; one congenital myopathy; 21 congenital hypotonia, not further classified; four postural immaturity; two degeneration of the central nervous system; one brain tumour; one spinal cord injury; two malnutrition and one scurvy. Of the 21 cases of congenital hypotonia, 19 were subsequently followed up: 13 became normal, five showed mental retardation and one athetosis. A positive family history of delay in walking or 'double-jointedness' was present in nine cases of congenital hypotonia.

TABLE 1.V

Classification of hypotonia: Jebsen et al. (1961)

1. *CNS diseases (excluding the anterior horn cell)*
   1. Brain damage (including cerebral palsy and mental deficiency)
   2. Mongolism
   3. Degenerative CNS diseases
   4. Cerebellar disease

2. *Motor unit diseases*
   1. Werdnig-Hoffmann's disease
   2. Polyneuritis of insidious onset
   3. Neonatal poliomyelitis
   4. Muscular dystrophy
   5. Polymyositis
   6. Myasthenia gravis
   7. 'Benign congenital hypotonia'

3. *Metabolic disorders*
   Cretinism, scurvy, rickets, malnutrition, storage diseases, infantile acidosis, infantile hypercalcaemia, adrenocortical hyperfunction, arachnoidactyly, osteogenesis imperfecta, prolonged debilitating states (*e.g.* chronic infection, heart disease)

Jebsen *et al.* (1961) suggested classification of the causes of hypotonia into three broad categories: (1) central nervous system diseases, (2) motor unit diseases and (3) metabolic disorders. These they further subdivided, as shown in Table 1.V.

Zellweger *et al.* (1962) divided the causes of hypotonia into two broad categories: (1) chemical and endocrine disturbances and (2) disturbances within the nervous system and neuromuscular apparatus. These they further subdivided, as in Table 1.VI. Rabe (1964) reviewed the causes of hypotonia within the neuromuscular system and subdivided them on an anatomical and pathological basis (Table 1.VII). It is of interest that the first two conditions which Rabe included under his section of hypotonia due to diseases of the muscle were benign congenital hypotonia and universal muscular hypoplasia, implying that these were 'diseases'.

TABLE 1.VI

Classification of hypotonia: Zellweger et al. (1962)

I. *Chemical and endocrine causes of muscular hypotonia*
  1. Alterations of the gradient of potassium inside and outside the membrane of the muscle cell with hypopotassemia, normopotassemia or hyperpotassemia
     (a) Familial periodic paralysis
     (b) Adynamia episodica hereditaria
     (c) Hyperaldosteronism and Cushing's syndrome
  2. Hypercalcemia
     (a) Idiopathic hypercalcemia
     (b) Hypervitaminosis D
     (c) Hyperparathyroidism
  3. Hypophosphatemia
     (a) Coeliac disease and other nutritional disorders
     (b) Different forms of rickets
  4. Hypomagnesemia
  5. Hyper- and hypofunction of the thyroid gland
  6. Neuronopathy due to:
     (a) Cortisone therapy
     (b) Hyperinsulinism
  7. Diabetic polyneuritis
  8. Panhypopituitarism

II. *Neuromuscular hypotonia*
  1. Cortical hypotonia
  2. Subcortical supraspinal hypotonia
     i.   Inherited degenerative and metabolic diseases:
          Spinocerebellar ataxia
          Some forms of diffuse demyelinization
          Early phases of cerebral lipidosis
          Mucopolysaccharidosis (some cases)
          Phenylketonuria (some cases)
     ii. Constitutional and chromosomal aberrations:
          Mongolism
          Turner's syndrome and pterygium disease
          Arachnodactyly (Marfan syndrome)
          Brachydactyly or acromicria
          Benign congenital hypotonia
     iii. Convulsive disorders and mental retardation:
          Idiopathic epilepsy
          Idiopathic infantile spasms
          Different forms of mental retardation
     iv. Peripheral reflex arc and muscle
          (a) its afferent branch
          (b) its efferent branch (lower motor neuron)
          (c) Muscle

8

The above classifications all presented a systematic approach, based on anatomical, pathological or biochemical criteria. In practice, this made them impractical in the clinical assessment of the floppy infant, since it meant excluding many rare conditions in a systematic fashion before considering the more common ones. In the next chapter I present a practical clinical approach to the diagnosis and classification of the floppy infant.

TABLE 1.VII

Causes of hypotonia within the neuromuscular system: Rabe (1964)

A. *Hypotonia due to diseases of the central nervous system*
    1. Atonic diplegia
    2. Congenital chorea and athetosis
    3. Congenital cerebellar ataxia
    4. Kernicterus
    5. Mongolism
    6. Tay-Sachs disease

B. *Hypotonia due to diseases of the spinal cord*
    1. Werdnig-Hoffmann's disease (infantile progressive muscular atrophy)
    2. Myelopathic arthrogryposis multiplex congenita
    3. Congenital anterior poliomyelitis

C. *Hypotonia due to diseases of the spinal roots or peripheral nerves*
    1. Acute and chronic polyneuropathy

D. *Hypotonia due to abnormalities of the myoneural junction*
    1. Congenital myasthenia gravis
    2. Neonatal (transient) myasthenia gravis

E. *Hypotonia due to diseases of the muscle*
    1. Benign congenital hypotonia
    2. Universal muscular hypoplasia
    3. Congenital infantile muscular dystrophy with or without arthrogryposis multiplex congenita
    4. Dystrophia myotonica
    5. Central core disease
    6. Rod body myopathy
    7. Polymyositis
    8. Glycogen storage disease

CHAPTER 2

A Practical Approach to the Diagnosis and Classification of the Floppy Infant

I do not intend to describe conventional history-taking and clinical examination of the infant in this monograph but would like to draw attention to some aspects of the clinical examination which will be most useful in the accurate assessment of hypotonia and in an understanding of the differential diagnosis of the floppy infant.

Assessment of hypotonia

The diagnosis of hypotonia may be a subjective impression to some extent, based on the 'feel' of the infant when handled, the resistance of a limb to passive movement, or the postures which the child adopts. Thus one readily recognizes the classical 'frog posture' of the floppy infant, with the hips in a position of abduction and external rotation and the limbs in contact with the surface on which the infant is lying, owing to the absence of any postural tone (Fig. 2.1). This is readily contrasted with the posture of flexion and adduction of the hips seen in the normal infant (Fig. 2.2).

Two positions are very helpful in the objective assessment of the floppy infant:

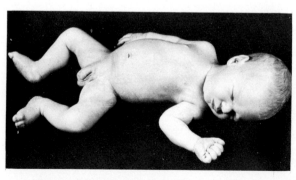
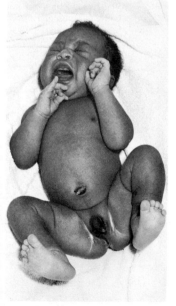

Fig. 2.1 *(left)*. Floppy infant supine; 'frog' posture (Werdnig-Hoffmann disease).
Fig. 2.2 *(right)*. Normal posture of full-term infant in supine, with flexion of hands and legs.

ventral suspension and traction on the hands in the supine position. In ventral suspension, with the infant supported prone by a hand under the chest, head control, trunk curvature and control of the arms and legs can be readily assessed. A normal full-term newborn infant will hold the head at about 45° or less to the horizontal, the back will be straight or only slightly flexed, the arms flexed at the elbows and partially extended at the shoulders, and the knees partially flexed (Fig. 2.3). Even an immature infant will show a variable degree of postural tone, depending on length of gestation (Fig. 2.4). The floppy infant, in contrast, will have marked head lag and floppiness of the trunk, arms and legs (Fig. 2.5).

In the supine position, traction on the hands to raise the shoulders off the couch will result in some degree of flexion of the head in full-term as well as immature infants. Many full-term infants can already keep the head in the same plane as the body (Fig. 2.6), and even in the preterm infant some head control is usually present from about 34 weeks gestation (Fig. 2.7). The floppy infant, in contrast, will show marked head lag (Fig. 2.8).

Assessment of the infant in these two positions is of value, irrespective of the cause of the hypotonia, and is useful in initial evaluation as well as for subsequent comparative assessments.

An additional response of value in the assessment of hypotonia in the newborn infant is the resistance of the flexor muscles of the elbow or knee in response to traction of the hand or foot respectively (Figs 2.9 and 2.10). Normally some resistance is present and flexion of some degree at the elbow or knee is maintained in response to extending the limb and trying to lift the shoulder or hip off the bed. In hypotonic infants there is diminished resistance with this manoeuvre.

Since hypotonia is a normal feature in the preterm infant, all assessment of tone in the newborn period must be related to the gestational maturity of the infant, so it is important for a detailed assessment of gestational age to be made prior to the assessment of neuromuscular function, particularly in a low-birthweight infant (Dubowitz *et al.* 1970, Dubowitz and Dubowitz 1977).

Traditional paediatric manoeuvres in the assessment of muscle function, such as palpation of muscles, are unrewarding, and I think likely to give a more accurate assessment of the amount of subcutaneous fat than of the functional state of the musculature.

The tendon reflexes are also of limited value in diagnosis. They are likely to be absent in Werdnig-Hoffmann's disease so that a normal or brisk response makes this diagnosis unlikely; but they may also be absent in other forms of hypotonia. Brisk reflexes may point to a diagnosis of the hypotonic form of cerebral palsy, which may become spastic as the child gets older, or to some of the other forms of hypotonia of central origin such as the Prader-Willi syndrome.

Differential diagnosis and classification

There may be certain advantages in approaching the differential diagnosis of the floppy infant on an anatomical basis (Fig. 2.11) as this provides a useful checklist of the various types of causative disorder or an approach to the mechanisms involved (Fig. 2.12).

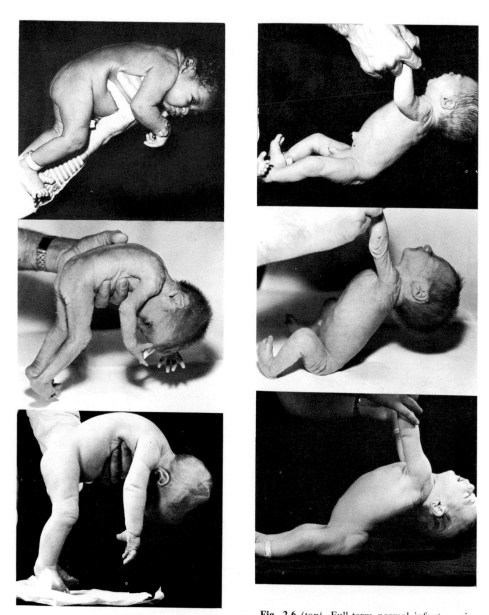

Fig. 2.3 *(top).* Normal infant in ventral suspension; flexed arms and legs, straight back, and head 45° or less to horizontal.
Fig. 2.4 *(centre).* Preterm infant of about 34 weeks gestation; some postural tone in trunk and limbs.
Fig. 2.5 *(bottom).* Floppy infant in ventral suspension; poor posture in trunk, arms and legs (Werdnig-Hoffmann disease).

Fig. 2.6 *(top).* Full-term normal infant, supine with hand traction.
Fig. 2.7 *(centre).* Preterm infant of about 34 weeks gestation; some postural control of head.
Fig. 2.8 *(bottom).* Floppy infant; marked head lag in supine with hand traction.

From a clinical point of view, in the assessment of the individual case it is more practical to apply a few simple clinical criteria in order to subdivide the cases into broad groups in the first instance. Further differentiation is then more logically undertaken and investigations can be based on the most likely diagnosis, rather than on a whole battery of screening tests.

The first two questions to be asked when confronted with a floppy baby are:
(1) Is this a weak or paralysed child with incidental hypotonia?
(2) Is this a hypotonic child without significant muscle weakness?
An answer to these questions will subdivide the cases into two broad groups: paralytic and non-paralytic. The distinction can usually be made by careful observation of the floppy infant in a supine position. If he is able to move his limbs against gravity, either spontaneously or following a stimulus to the soles or the hands, or if he is able to maintain the posture of a passively elevated limb, he does not have significant weakness.

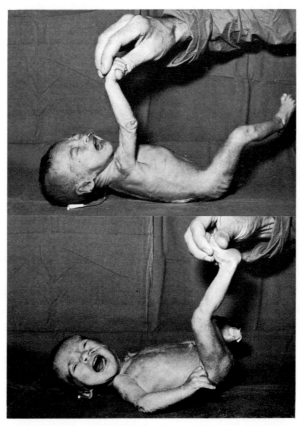

Fig. 2.9 *(top).* One-week-old infant of 35 weeks gestation: flexor tone with hand traction.
Fig. 2.10 *(bottom).* Same infant shows flexor tone in knee on foot traction.

13

In the *paralytic group* the most common cause is infantile spinal muscular atrophy (Werdnig-Hoffmann's disease). Other causes are the various congenital myopathies and other neuromuscular disorders (see classification, Table 2.I). In the table I have attempted to list the various conditions in the order of frequency with which they are likely to present in the neonatal period or early infancy.

In the *non-paralytic group*, in which hypotonia is the predominant symptom, there is a wide variety of possible causes. The largest sub-group comprises diseases of the central nervous system, particularly in association with mental retardation. It is

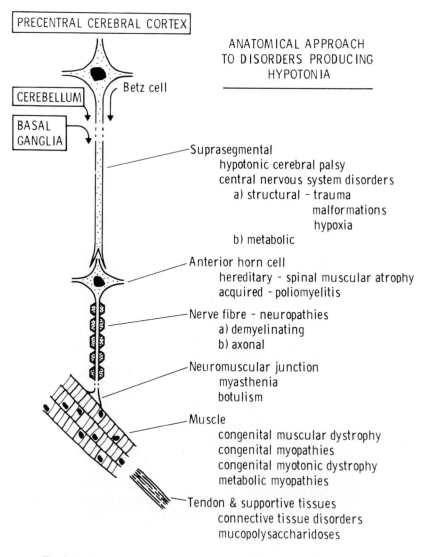

Fig. 2.11. Anatomical approach to the causes of the floppy infant syndrome.

thus important to try to decide whether the child is mentally retarded in addition to being hypotonic. This may be difficult in the early weeks of life. Some indication of abnormality of the central nervous system may be suspected because of the poor state of alertness of the infant, lack of response to visual and auditory stimuli, or inability to manage co-ordinated functions such as sucking and swallowing (Dubowitz and Dubowitz, 1980, Dubowitz *et al.* 1980). A careful history of events in the perinatal period may also help to determine whether any specific event such as birth asphyxia may have been a factor.

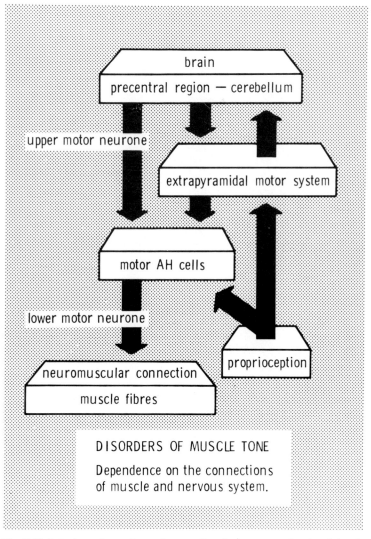

Fig. 2.12. Interdependence of neural connections between central and peripheral nervous systems in maintenance of muscle tone. (After Hertl 1977, p. 532.)

TABLE 2.I

Paralytic conditions with incidental hypotonia

(1) *Hereditary infantile spinal muscular atrophy*
        Werdnig-Hoffmann disease
        Benign variants

(2) *Congenital myopathies*
        Structural: Central core disease
                    Minicore disease
                    Nemaline myopathy
                    Myotubular myopathy
                    Myotubular myopathy with type 1 fibre hypotrophy
                    Myotubular myopathy, X-linked
                    Mixed myopathies
                    Congenital fibre type disproportion
                    Mitochondrial myopathies
                    Other subcellular abnormalities
                    'Minimal change myopathy'
        Metabolic: Glycogenosis types II, III, (IV)
                    Lipid storage myopathy
                    Periodic paralysis

(3) *Other neuromuscular disorders*
        Congenital myotonic dystrophy
        Congenital muscular dystrophy
        Neonatal myasthenia; congenital myasthenia
        Motor neuropathies
        Other neuromuscular disorders

TABLE 2.II

Non-paralytic conditions: hypotonia without significant weakness

(1) *Disorders affecting the central nervous system*
        Non-specific mental deficiency
        Hypotonic cerebral palsy
        Birth trauma, intracranial haemorrhage, intrapartum asphyxia and hypoxia
        Chromosomal disorders; Down's syndrome
        Metabolic disorders: aminoacidurias; organic acidurias; sphingolipidoses (leucodystrophies)

(2) *Connective tissue disorders*
        Congenital laxity of ligaments
        Ehlers-Danlos and Marfan syndromes
        Osteogenesis imperfecta
        Mucopolysaccharidoses

(3) *Prader-Willi syndrome* (hypotonia-obesity)

(4) *Metabolic, nutritional, endocrine*
        renal tubular acidosis; hypercalcaemia; rickets, coeliac disease; hyptothyroidism

(5) *Benign congenital hypotonia.* (Essential hypotonia)

Many infants in this group are likely to present after the neonatal period with a delay in achieving motor milestones and associated hypotonia. It should then be fairly easy to establish whether other milestones not dependent on motor activity, such as smiling, vocalization, social response, following objects with the eyes are also delayed. It is also helpful to try to assess whether the delay in intellectual milestones is commensurate with the motor delay or is disproportionately more marked.

Hypotonia may be associated with mental deficiency with no apparent underlying disease process, or may occur in association with specific and recognizable disorders such as Down's syndrome, cerebral lipidoses and other degenerative disorders of the nervous system, some forms of cerebral palsy, microcephaly and so forth. The hypotonia may be proportionate to the degree of mental subnormality, but in some of these conditions there may be gross hypotonia with only minimal mental retardation. Until more is known about the pathogenesis of hypotonia, it will be difficult to understand this apparently non-specific relationship of hypotonia to mental retardation.

Hypotonia may also be symptomatic of many other conditions affecting various systems of the body, the more common of which are listed in the classification in Table 2.II. The connective tissue disorders probably constitute the largest group among these, and as many of them are genetically determined, a careful family history and examination of the parents may help to pinpoint the diagnosis. Hypotonia may be a striking feature of many of the metabolic disorders presenting either in the newborn period or later, but there are usually other associated features which provide a clue to the nature of the underlying disorder.

Finally, there is a small residuum of cases with hypotonia as an isolated feature and with *no apparent underlying muscle weakness, intellectual retardation or associated disease.* I think that if the term 'benign congenital hypotonia' or 'essential hypotonia' is to be used at all, it should be restricted to this group in which the muscle power is normal and electrodiagnostic studies and muscle biopsy (if done) reveal no abnormality, and in which there is no apparent associated cause. The cases with associated weakness, even of a non-progressive type, will probably turn out to be one or other form of neuromuscular disorder, particularly the newly recognized congenital myopathies or the milder forms of spinal muscular atrophy, and should be categorized as such rather than having a label of benign hypotonia.

A number of cases that I originally designated as 'benign congenital hypotonia' and subsequently followed up turned out to be examples of the Prader-Willi syndrome (Dubowitz 1963). This illustrates the importance of the associated features, such as swallowing difficulty, unusual facies, or the subsequent association of intellectual retardation which may not be apparent in the immediate newborn period.

In many of the non-paralytic group of cases the underlying disorder may be obvious. Many of the cases in the literature which have resulted in this expanding list of potential causes of the floppy infant syndrome have in fact been well-defined cases of a specific syndrome in which the hypotonia was an incidental and insignificant feature. The main disorders which are likely to present with hypotonia as a predominant feature are the central nervous system disorders and the disorders of connective tissue. Some of the metabolic disorders may also have profound hypotonia

17

as a presenting feature and in some an element of muscle weakness may also be apparent.

Some overlap is bound to occur between the paralytic group and the non-paralytic group since some floppy infants with marked hypotonia may also have a minor degree of associated weakness which may not be clinically striking, or may appear to be weak whereas in fact the power of the muscle is reasonable but is overshadowed by profound hypotonia. The latter may occur, for example, in the Prader-Willi syndrome, but in general the two groups will be readily distinguishable and one should base the assessment predominantly on the degree of hypotonia in relation to the amount of apparent weakness. In the neuromuscular disorders, the weakness will usually be apparent in proportion to the hypotonia, whereas in the conditions with symptomatic hypotonia in relation to disorders of other systems the hypotonia will be disproportionately marked in comparison with any apparent associated weakness.

PART I

PARALYTIC DISORDERS

Muscular Weakness with Incidental Hypotonia. Neuromuscular Disorders

CHAPTER 3

Spinal Muscular Atrophies

The severe form of spinal muscular atrophy is the commonest cause of hypotonia with associated muscle weakness. The clinical course and prognosis of this condition has not changed, despite the advent of antibiotics, and these infants still die in early infancy from associated pneumonia, a common complication because of the paralysed intercostal muscles.

Advances over the past two decades in our understanding of the variations in clinical severity of spinal muscular atrophy have helped to clarify much of the confusion in diagnosis which occurred in the past.

Although the severe infantile form of spinal muscular atrophy carries the eponymous title of Werdnig-Hoffmann disease, in the two cases described by Werdnig and the five by Hoffmann the onset of weakness was in the second half of the first year of life, and they survived to between 14 months and six years of age. Some of them would now be categorized more appropriately in the intermediate severity group (see below). Brandt (1950) and Byers and Banker (1961) drew attention to the varying severity of the disease and noted that in general the earlier the onset, the more severe and precipitous the course.

Infantile spinal muscular atrophy (Werdnig-Hoffmann's disease)

Clinical features

The severe form of infantile spinal muscular atrophy shows a very typical and consistent clinical pattern.

Onset. The onset is early, either *in utero* or within the first two or three months of life. The onset may often appear to be abrupt and a previously active child rapidly becomes paralysed and immobile. This may be noted by the mother *in utero* as a sudden cessation of previously strong fetal movements. More often, however, there is no antenatal warning and the condition presents unexpectedly at birth. The youngest infant I have seen was a 32-week gestation, preterm infant with marked hypotonia from birth and classical features of spinal muscular atrophy when assessed at four weeks.

In those infants with onset after birth, the paralysis may also appear acutely, without any previous sign of weakness. This was well illustrated by one of my patients. Since a sibling had previously died of Werdnig-Hoffmann's disease at the age of six months, I carefully examined this child at birth. The power in the limbs and trunk was normal, as were all the neonatal reflexes and tendon jerks. Daily assessment during the first 10 days in hospital revealed no abnormality. However, when he returned to the clinic for routine follow-up at six weeks he had severe paralysis. This had come on abruptly at four weeks of age. He showed little further progression of weakness, and died of pneumonia at six months. Occasional severe cases have onset beyond three months of age, but in general these later cases tend to be milder in severity.

Clinical picture. The infant usually shows a very characteristic clinical picture. There is marked generalized weakness and hypotonia, and in supine the infant will usually lie in a characteristic 'frog posture' with abduction and external rotation of the legs (Fig. 3.1). The legs are more severely affected than the arms, and proximal muscles more than distal. The legs are frequently almost totally immobile except for some movement of the toes and feet. The arms may be a little more mobile, with ability to move the hands and to flex and extend the elbows, but the infant is usually unable to raise the arms against gravity.

The trunk is also severely affected and there is marked head lag both in ventral suspension and in supine with arm traction (Figs. 3.2, 3.3). These infants are never able to raise their heads or to roll over.

The face is strikingly spared and the infant usually has a bright, alert expression (Fig. 3.1) which contrasts with the general paralysis. The infant acquires the ability to smile at a normal age.

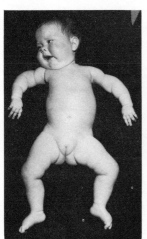

Fig. 3.1

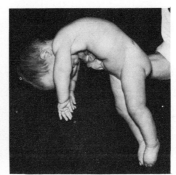

Fig. 3.2

Fig. 3.3

Fig. 3.1. Six-week-old infant with severe infantile SMA: 'frog' posture of limbs in supine.
Fig. 3.2. Same infant; marked hypotonia in ventral suspension.
Fig. 3.3. Same infant; marked head lag and 'frog' posture of legs with traction on hands.

21

Bulbar and respiratory muscles are affected and there is frequent difficulty with sucking and swallowing, associated with pooling of secretions in the pharynx. There is also associated respiratory distress and, with the marked intercostal weakness, breathing is mainly diaphragmatic. This gives the characteristic bell-shaped chest, with marked intercostal recession and corresponding abdominal distension with inspiration (Fig. 3.4). The infant's cry is often weak, high-pitched and ineffectual, as is any effort at coughing.

Fasciculation may be noted in the tongue but often is difficult to distinguish from tremor. There is no atrophy of the tongue and no fasciculation of the skeletal muscles. Sometimes a tremor of the hands is noted, which may subsequently disappear.

The tendon reflexes are always absent and their presence should raise suspicion of an alternative diagnosis.

Contractures. Severe contractures as seen in 'arthrogryposis' are not a feature of spinal muscular atrophy, but mild contractures are common and occur early. The adductors of the hips are usually affected, with resultant limitation of abduction (Fig. 3.5). There may also be a few degrees of fixed flexion of the knees. The shoulders typically have contractures of the internal rotators, giving the characteristic 'jug-handle' or 'seal-flipper' postural deformity of the arms (Fig. 3.5). On rare occasions there may be flexion deformities of the hands and fingers.

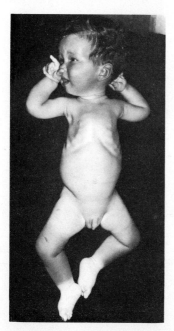 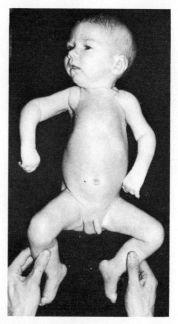

Fig. 3.4 *(left).* Severe infantile SMA; bell-shaped chest with marked costal recession, diaphragmatic breathing and abdominal distension.
Fig. 3.5 *(right).* Infantile SMA; limitation of hip abduction and 'jug-handle' posture of arms.

Course and prognosis

These severe cases with early onset rarely survive the first year of life, owing to the risk of intercurrent pneumonia and respiratory failure. Indeed the most severe cases with marked respiratory involvement may not even survive the first few months of life (Fig. 3.6). The main factor in prognosis for survival, irrespective of the degree of weakness of the limbs, is the extent of respiratory and bulbar involvement. In a recent study of respiratory function in infants with Werdnig-Hoffmann's disease, we found that those with intra-uterine onset tend to have reduced lung volume compared with those with postnatal onset, suggesting that the intercostal paralysis *in utero* may also influence normal lung development (Cunningham and Stocks 1978). Cardiac muscle is not affected.

Despite the classical description of the progressive nature of spinal muscular atrophy, in my experience the muscle weakness is often surprisingly non-progressive and many of these infants with very limited residual power in the arms or legs seem to retain this power throughout their short life (Fig. 3.7). This is comparable to the non-progressive character of the more benign forms (see below) and suggests that there may be some precipitating factor causing the onset of the weakness, which rapidly reaches its peak and then stays on the same plateau. Even within this severe group there is some variability in clinical severity and prognosis, and some cases have reasonably good lung function and are likely to survive somewhat longer as a result.

Diagnosis

One can usually make the clinical diagnosis with some degree of confidence, but confirmation is always essential in view of the poor prognosis and also for genetic counselling. Electrodiagnostic studies may give supportive findings. Motor nerve conduction velocity is frequently difficult to measure, especially in the legs, owing to the characteristically poor response of the muscle to stimulation. The velocity is often slow in the severe form. Electromyography may show spontaneous fibrillation potentials at rest and a reduced interference pattern on voluntary contraction. Muscle biopsy is the only certain method of confirmation and shows a characteristic picture of large groups, frequently whole bundles, of uniformly atrophic fibres interspersed with single or groups of normal-sized or enlarged fibres (Fig. 3.8). These large fibres

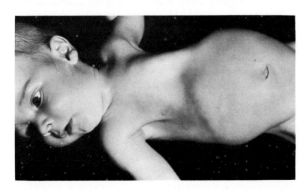

Fig. 3.6. Three-month-old infant with severe infantile SMA: marked respiratory deficit with intercostal paralysis and reduction in chest size. (Note alert, expressive face.)

23

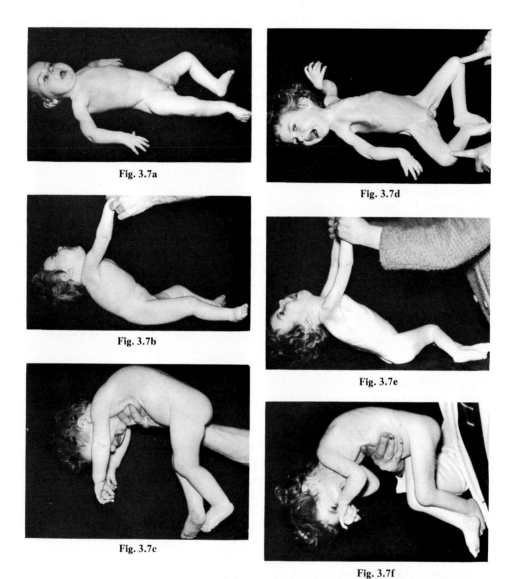

Fig. 3.7a

Fig. 3.7d

Fig. 3.7b

Fig. 3.7e

Fig. 3.7c

Fig. 3.7f

Fig. 3.7a, b, c. Six-month-old infant with severe infantile SMA, onset at four months of age. 'Frog' posture in supine, with limited hip abduction beyond 70°; marked hypotonia and poor head and limb control in supine and in ventral suspension.

Fig. 3.7d, e, f. Same infant 15 months later. General weight loss and marked deterioration in respiratory function, but no appreciable change in posture or in power in trunk and limbs.

24

are usually of one uniform histochemical type, suggesting they may be reinnervated fibres, presumably resulting from the sprouting of surviving axons, which then reinnervate adjacent denervated fibres. One cannot give any opinion of severity or prognosis from the histological picture, as an identical pattern occurs in the more benign variants of spinal muscular atrophy.

Muscle biopsy in the very early stages of the disease, within a few weeks of onset, may show an unusual picture of a fairly normal-looking pattern except for the universally small size of the muscle fibres and that type 1 fibres appear to be smaller than the type 2. This should not be confused with congenital fibre-type disproportion (in which the type 2 fibres are normal in size, or enlarged): it represents a 'pre-pathological' stage of spinal atrophy when the muscle is still undergoing extensive denervation and has not yet become reinnervated by surviving neurones. These cases later show the classical biopsy picture of spinal atrophy (Dubowitz 1978). Serum creatine phosphokinase is normal in severe infantile spinal muscular atrophy but may be elevated in some cases of the milder forms.

At autopsy there are extensive degenerative changes in the anterior horn cells of the cord and the nuclei of the motor cranial nerves. Heart muscle is unaffected.

Management

These infants present a difficult problem of management: with bulbar and respiratory weakness they often need tube feeding (gavage) and frequent pharyngeal aspiration. Inhalation of feeds and collapse of parts of the lung are common and, in view of the poor over-all prognosis, do not warrant heroic measures at resuscitation. One should avoid putting these infants on a ventilator for their respiratory failure as it will almost inevitably be impossible to take them off the ventilator again. Similarly, general anaesthesia for an attempt at bronchial lavage for partial lung collapse may leave the infant worse off rather than better.

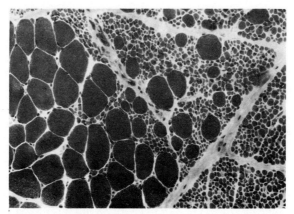

Fig. 3.8. Muscle biopsy of patient with infantile SMA. Classical picture of group atrophy with large clusters (often whole bundles) of uniformly atrophic fibres, interspersed with isolated fibres or groups of normal-sized or enlarged fibres, which are reinnervated fibres of uniform histochemical type.

Genetics

Spinal muscular atrophy is inherited through an autosomal recessive mechanism. In the severe form there is usually concordance among affected sibs (Pearn *et al.* 1973) but one does come across families in which one (or more) children may have spinal muscular atrophy of intermediate severity and another child die with the severe form (Dubowitz 1964).

There is no way of detecting heterozygotes, and as yet no possibility of prenatal diagnosis. It seems unlikely that a method of prenatal diagnosis of spinal muscular atrophy in the second trimester of pregnancy will be possible in the future unless some specific genetic marker of the disease can be identified.

Benign variants

Some patients with spinal muscular atrophy, particularly of later onset, may survive infancy and even reach their teens and adolescence. They mainly present with delay in motor milestones, and hypotonia and muscle weakness are essential clinical features. The weakness is usually non-progressive and in general these children retain the motor skills they have acquired prior to the onset of weakness.

As in Werdnig-Hoffmann's disease, proximal muscles are more severely affected than distal and the legs more than the arms. Trunk muscles are also affected but the face is spared. In the most benign forms the child achieves the ability to walk, and the weakness may be confined to the proximal pelvic-girdle muscles.

There have been numerous attempts to define specific genetic entities and clinical syndromes, based mainly on the age at onset of the condition and the length of survival. In practice these are both impractical, and in the individual case I have found a simple classification based on the clinical severity, irrespective of age of onset, to be a practical and useful approach. Based on the infant's ability to sit or stand, one can recognize three clear-cut forms: (1) *Severe*—unable to sit unsupported (Werdnig-Hoffmann's disease); (2) *Intermediate*—able to sit unsupported, unable to stand or walk unaided; (3) *Mild*—able to stand or walk (Kugelberg-Welander syndrome). Within each group there is a spectrum of severity, thus ranging over-all from very severe to very mild. The mild form usually presents after the child starts walking and need not concern us here. The intermediate form, on the other hand, frequently presents as a floppy infant and was one of the main diagnostic problems and causes of confusion in the past.

Intermediate severity spinal muscular atrophy

Onset is usually insidious. The typical history is of a child progressing quite normally during the first six months or so and attaining the usual motor milestones and ability to sit unaided. The child is then unable to take weight on his legs and is unable to stand or walk. The apparent onset of symptoms is thus between six and 18 months of age. In some instances the parents notice a fairly rapid onset of weakness in the legs, with loss of previous mobility, but in others there is no clear-cut point of onset and in retrospect the parents may have suspected diminished movement of the legs since the first months of life, occasionally even since birth.

26

Clinical picture. The child is usually able to sit well and to pivot. The legs show symmetrical weakness affecting proximal muscles more than distal. In some the weakness is fairly marked and they adopt a frog posture, as in the severe form (Fig. 3.9), whereas in others the power may be reasonably good and they are almost able to take their weight on the legs (Figs 3.10 and 3.11). Similarly, the weakness in the arms varies from almost negligible, with ability to raise the arms (Fig. 3.9), to fairly marked weakness of the shoulder girdle and inability to raise the arms against gravity.

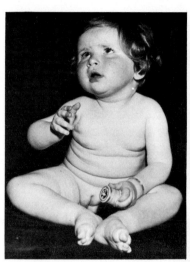

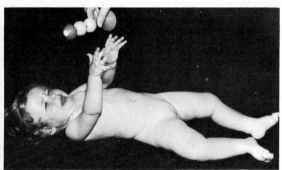

Fig. 3.9b

Fig. 3.9a

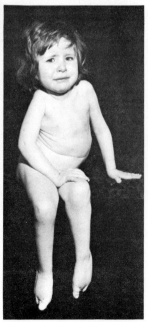

Fig. 3.9c

Fig. 3.9. Eighteen-month-old child with intermediate-severity SMA: *(a)* able to sit unaided; *(b)* marked flaccidity and 'frog' posture of legs; and *(c)* marked progression of scoliosis 18 months later.

27

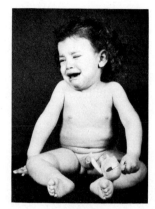

Fig. 3.10a

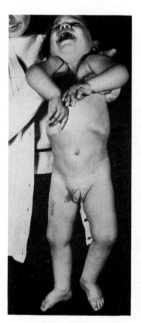

Fig. 3.10b

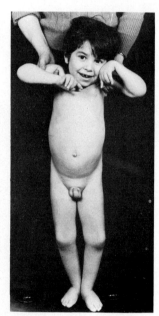

Fig. 3.10c

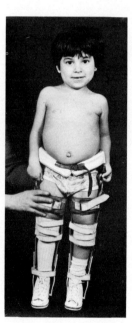

Fig. 3.10d

Fig. 3.10. Two-year-old child with intermediate-severity SMA: *(a)* stable sitting posture; and *(b)* able to take some weight on legs but unable to stand unsupported. Same child at 4½ years is still unable to stand unsupported *(c)* but is able to stand and walk with full-length calipers with pelvic support *(d)*.

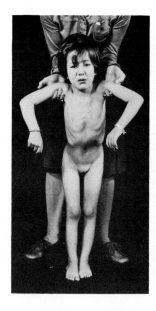

Fig. 3.11. Five-year-old girl with intermediate-severity SMA who had had
bilateral open reduction of dislocated hips:
unable to stand unsupported *(left)*, but
able to stand and walk unaided after
fitting of lightweight moulded polyethylene
ishcial-bearing calipers, without a pelvic
band *(right)*.

There are no bulbar symptoms, but fasciculation and atrophy of the tongue are a
common feature. The face is not affected. The intercostal muscles are usually not
appreciably affected but some cases may show marked intercostal weakness and
mainly diaphragmatic breathing, as in the severe form. There is usually no visible
fasciculation of skeletal muscles but a coarse tremor of the hands, which may be
transitory, is common (Moosa and Dubowitz 1973) and the electrocardiogram shows
a characteristic tremulousness of the baseline, particularly in the limb leads, which
presumably reflects the same underlying muscle tremor (Fig. 3.12). The tendon
reflexes are absent or markedly depressed. These children are of normal or above
average intelligence.

Course and prognosis

The course is usually benign, with survival into adolescence and adult life, and
the muscle power tends to remain static (Fig. 3.13). Some may even show apparent
improvement in muscle function, presumably from reinnervation of muscle or better
use of existing muscles. Some patients may show deterioration in power, either
spasmodically or steadily.

Prognosis for survival is dependent on respiratory function, and those with
intercostal weakness and recurrent pneumonia have a poor outlook. Usually cardiac
muscle is not involved.

Deformities

As a result of being chairbound and having associated weakness of the trunk
muscles, from an early age these children are prone to develop scoliosis, which can be
very rapidly progressive (Fig. 3.8). They also tend to develop flexion contractures in
the hips, knees and elbows in relation to the habitual posture of the limbs.

29

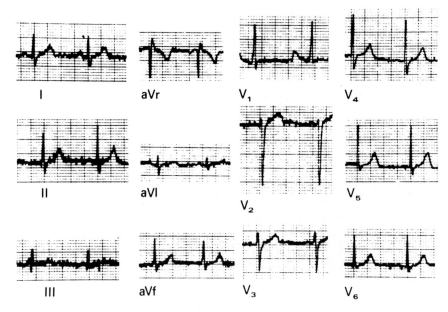

Fig. 3.12. Electrocardiogram of child with intermediate SMA, showing tremulous baseline, especially over the limb leads, which is a common (?invariable) feature of intermediate SMA, but not usually present in severe SMA.

Diagnosis

Serum creatine phosphokinase is usually normal but may be moderately elevated. Nerve conduction velocity is normal. Electromyography shows evidence of denervation, with fibrillation potentials at rest, large polyphasic potentials on volition and a reduced interference pattern. Muscle biopsy shows a typical picture of atrophy of large groups of fibres of both histochemical types, interspersed with isolated or groups of large fibres of uniform histochemical activity (usually type 1) (Fig. 3.14). The picture is similar to that of the severe form of spinal muscular atrophy.

Management

From an early stage it is important to prevent deformity, as this may ultimately decide whether the child is going to become ambulant or not. The back should be closely watched and at the first suggestion of scoliosis developing an adequate spinal brace should be fitted. Ideally it may be worth bracing these children *before* the onset of scoliosis and thus ensure a straight back. Once scoliosis develops it may be very difficult to control and may need a Milwaukee type brace to get adequate reduction of the scoliosis while it is still mobile. At a later stage, one may have to consider spinal fusion in cases with severe scoliosis which one cannot arrest. This is usually deferred to eight or 10 years of age.

Passive movements of the limbs in order to take the joints through a full range of movement will help to prevent contractures. This is important in relation to the later fitting of callipers for ambulation. For those who have sufficient power in their arms

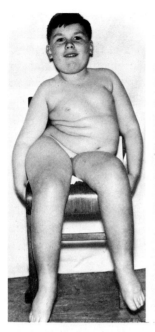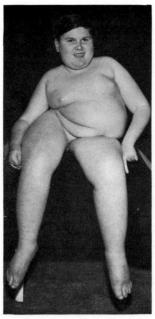

Fig. 3.13. Nine-year-old boy *(left)* with non-progressive SMA of intermediate severity who had been able to sit unaided by 12 months but was never able to stand or walk. 15-year follow-up has shown no appreciable deterioration in function at 14 years *(centre)* or 24 years *(right)*. The severe scoliosis, which started in early infancy, might have been preventable with bracing in infancy when the back was still straight.

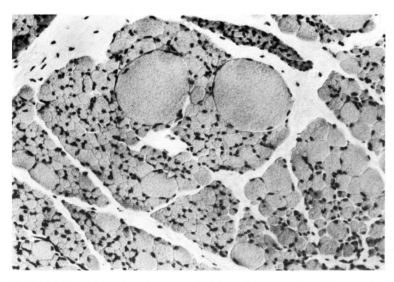

Fig. 3.14. Muscle biopsy from three-year-old child with SMA of intermediate severity shows uniform atrophy of large groups of fibres, interspersed with normal or enlarged fibres. Note the similarity with severe SMA (Fig. 3.8). Severity of histological change varies from one part of the biopsy to another and bears no relation to clinical severity.

31

to use sticks for supporting themselves, and who have some residual power in the legs, it is usually worth trying to get them ambulant with lightweight long-leg calipers (Figs 3.10, 3.11). They usually need a pelvic band as well because of marked weakness of the hip muscles. It is also worth actively trying to promote ambulation in these children, since the muscle power is usually stable and once they become ambulant there is a good chance they will continue to walk with their calipers. Exceptional cases may even improve to walking without calipers.

Genetics

As in the severe form of spinal muscular atrophy, inheritance is usually by an autosomal recessive mechanism. Affected siblings may show considerable variation in severity within the intermediate type, and one occasionally sees the concurrence within the same family of a severe or a mild case with an intermediate case (Dubowitz 1964, 1978).

There have been a number of reports of dominantly inherited spinal muscular atrophy, usually of a mild form and affected patients being ambulant. It is important to measure motor nerve conduction velocity in such cases to exclude the dominantly inherited demyelinating type of hereditary motor neuropathy (see below under 'other neuromuscular disorders').

X-linked inheritance has also been documented in occasional families.

CHAPTER 4

Congenital Myopathies

With the more enthusiastic investigation of muscle biopsies over the past few years by the modern techniques of histochemistry and electronmicroscopy, there has emerged out of the former morass of non-specific diagnostic labels—such as 'amyotonia congenita', 'universal muscle hypoplasia' and 'benign congenital hypotonia'—a series of myopathies with clearly delineated structural changes in the muscle. The descriptive titles given to these disorders have largely reflected the underlying pathological change in the muscle.

The generic term 'congenital myopathies' is useful and reasonably descriptive, although they are not all strictly congenital, with development *in utero* and symptoms at birth, and some may present very much later. The different entities cannot be diagnosed on clinical grounds alone, since they all tend to present either as a floppy infant syndrome or with non-progressive muscle weakness. In some the weakness is mainly proximal, in others fairly diffuse; some are very mildly affected and hardly incapacitated, others have severe and even life-threatening weakness. With increasing experience over the past few years a more consistent association of certain features with some of the syndromes can be recognized, making a clinical suspicion of specific entities more feasible. In addition, some of these conditions are more likely to present at birth or in early infancy with a floppy infant syndrome, whereas others more frequently tend to present later.

In the first edition of this monograph I suggested subdividing these congenital myopathies into those with 'structural changes' in the muscle and those with a recognizable biochemical defect. I think this is still a useful approach, although some entities such as the mitochondrial myopathies which are recognized on the basis of their structural abnormality, are now hovering on the verge of the metabolic group as a result of advances in the recognition of some of the specific metabolic abnormalities within the respiratory enzyme chain. Undoubtedly the structural changes in the mitochondria are secondary to an underlying metabolic abnormality and the same may well apply to many of the other forms of structural myopathy.

Clinical features

While all these syndromes present in a fairly non-specific way as floppy infants, the association of certain specific features may provide a clue to diagnosis. Thus involvement of the external ocular muscles occurs particularly with myotubular myopathy and mitochondrial myopathies, severe respiratory problems with myotubular myopathy (often with associated chest deformity) and nemaline myopathy, sucking and swallowing difficulties with myotubular myopathy and nemaline myopathy. Figure 4.1 shows a general differential diagnosis of neuromuscular disorders on the basis of some of these additional features.

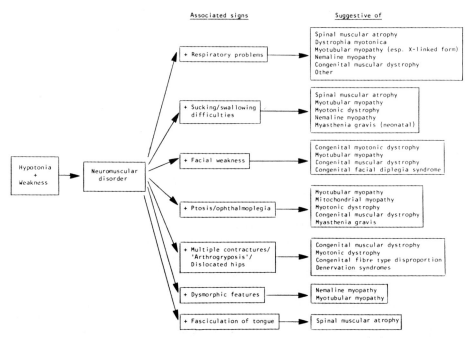

Associated signs
Suggestive of

+ Respiratory problems
Spinal muscular atrophy
Dystrophia myotonica
Myotubular myopathy (esp. X-linked form)
Nemaline myopathy
Congenital muscular dystrophy
Other

+ Sucking/swallowing difficulties
Spinal muscular atrophy
Myotubular myopathy
Myotonic dystrophy
Nemaline myopathy
Myasthenia gravis (neonatal)

+ Facial weakness
Congenital myotonic dystrophy
Myotubular myopathy
Congenital muscular dystrophy
Congenital facial diplegia syndrome

+ Ptosis/ophthalmoplegia
Myotubular myopathy
Mitochondrial myopathy
Myotonic dystrophy
Congenital muscular dystrophy
Myasthenia gravis

+ Multiple contractures/ 'Arthrogryposis'/ Dislocated hips
Congenital muscular dystrophy
Myotonic dystrophy
Congenital fibre type disproportion
Denervation syndromes

+ Dysmorphic features
Nemaline myopathy
Myotubular myopathy

+ Fasciculation of tongue
Spinal muscular atrophy

Hypotonia + Weakness → Neuromuscular disorder

Fig. 4.1. Flow diagram for differential diagnosis of hypotonia and weakness in the neonate, on the basis of associated features.

Investigations

Serum creatine phosphokinase and electromyography are not likely to be of much help in the diagnosis. CPK is usually normal, and a markedly raised level in an infant floppy from birth suggests a congenital muscular dystrophy (see below). Nerve conduction velocity is normal and electromyography is often normal but may show a mildly myopathic pattern with low-amplitude polyphasic potentials. Muscle biopsy is the only certain way of making an accurate diagnosis, and a full complement of histochemical techniques and electronmicroscopy is essential since the abnormalities frequently are not apparent on routine histological stains.

Despite fully comprehensive investigation, some cases with unequivocal weakness may show no apparent pathological change in the muscle. These presumably have as yet unrecognizable structural or biochemical abnormality. Some cases may show minimal myopathic change, with variability in fibre size but little other change. I have suggested the term 'minimal change myopathy' for these cases (Dubowitz 1978). Some of them may well be mild cases of congenital muscular dystrophy.

The following is a list of the congenital myopathies recognized to date.
  (1) Central core disease
  (2) Minicore disease (multicore disease)
  (3) Nemaline myopathy ('rod body' myopathy)
  (4) *a)* Myotubular myopathy (centronuclear myopathy)
      b) Myotubular myopathy with type 1 fibre hypotrophy

34

(5) Mixed myopathies

(6) Congenital fibre type disproportion

(7) Congenital type 1 fibre predominance

(8) Mitochondrial myopathies

(9) Other subcellular abnormalities

(10) Non-specific congenital myopathies; 'minimal change myopathy'

With the wider investigation of floppy infants, more myopathies will undoubtedly be described in the future. While some of these conditions, such as the X-linked myotubular myopathy, seem more likely to present as a severe floppy infant syndrome at birth, any attempt to subdivide them into those likely to present in early infancy or later is arbitrary, since in all of them there seems to be a marked variability in the clinical severity as well as the age at apparent onset of weakness.

A. 'STRUCTURAL' CONGENITAL MYOPATHIES

Central core disease

In 1956 Shy and Magee described a 'new congenital non-progressive myopathy' affecting five patients, four male and one female, in three generations of the same family. Their ages ranged from two to 65 years. The disease was present at birth or shortly after and in one case there was a history of reduced fetal movements. Early features were delay in achieving motor milestones and bizarre postures. The older patients had not walked until four or five years of age and still had residual difficulty in climbing stairs, running or rising from a supine or sitting posture. The two affected children, aged two and four years, walked at 14 and 20 months respectively but still had difficulty going up stairs, running or rising from the supine, which they did with the Gowers manoeuvre. There was associated hypotonia. In the older patients the condition remained fairly static over the years.

Histologically, the muscle was characterized by amorphous-looking central areas within the muscle fibres, composed of compact myofibrils giving a blue stain with Gomori's trichrome, in contrast to the normal red-staining outer fibrils. Greenfield *et al.* (1958) subsequently suggested the name 'central core disease'.

A second case was documented by Engel *et al.* (1961). This 19-year-old male had been 'double-jointed' in infancy but not floppy. His motor milestones were delayed and although he walked at two years he preferred to crawl or shuffle on his bottom till about four years. He had had difficulty in physically keeping up with his fellows at school, and still had difficulty in getting up from the supine or sitting positions and in going up steps. He was able to walk an unlimited distance on the level without fatigue or cramps.

Histochemical studies of this case showed the cores to be devoid of enzyme activity and presumably a non-functioning part of the muscle (Dubowitz and Pearse 1960*a*). The cores were not necessarily central and many fibres had multiple cores. The muscle also had only type 1 fibres. In longitudinal section, the cores ran the length of the fibre. The parents of this patient showed a normal subdivision of muscle into fibre types, with no cores. Electronmicroscopy showed a virtual absence of mitochondria and sarcoplasmic reticulum in the core region, a marked reduction in the interfibrillary space and an irregular zig-zag pattern (streaming) of the Z lines (Engel *et al.* 1961, Seitelberger *et al.* 1961).

Clinical features

There have been several reports of central core disease since the initial cases, and in most instances the clinical pattern has been very similar to the original reports. The usual clinical presentation is one of a mild and relatively non-progressive muscle weakness, either proximal or generalized, and presenting either in early infancy or later. Armstrong *et al.* (1971) and Ramsey and Hensinger (1975) drew attention to the frequent association of congenital dislocation of the hip.

As has happened in so many of the other congenital myopathies, unusual cases presenting at a later age but with similar histopathology have been described, such as the unusual family of Bethlem *et al.* (1966) in which there were three affected females in successive generations with non-progressive proximal weakness and muscle cramps on exercise.

Genetics

The most consistent pattern of inheritance has been autosomal dominant. Other cases have apparently been sporadic. In view of the variability in clinical severity of the condition, it is probably important to carefully assess the parents of any isolated affected child and perhaps even to do muscle biopsies in apparently normal parents to exclude a possible dominant mechanism.

Histopathology

The cores seem to have a predilection for type 1 fibres. In some cases the muscle is composed entirely or almost entirely of type 1 fibres (Dubowitz and Pearse 1960*b*, Gonatas *et al.* 1965, Dubowitz and Roy 1970), whereas in others the muscle may appear to be differentiated in two fibre types but with type 1 fibres still selectively affected (Dubowitz and Platts 1965, Bethlem *et al.* 1966, Dubowitz and Roy 1970). A recent follow-up biopsy in the child reported by Dubowitz and Roy (1970) (Fig. 4.2), who has remained clinically static over the years, showed a remarkable change from a differentiated muscle with selective involvement of type 1 fibres in a small proportion of fibres only, to total lack of differentiation of the muscle, type 1 fibres only being present, and almost universal involvement of the fibres by central cores, as in the original biopsy of his mother. This suggests that the pathological process may continue to evolve after birth without any apparent progression of muscle weakness.

On electronmicroscopy, the cores show a structured pattern which is often out of phase with the rest of the muscle (Fig. 4.2) and an absence of mitochondria or sarcotubular structures. In addition to these so-called 'structured' cores, Neville and Brooke (1973) have also recognized cases in which the structure is apparently distorted and lost—the so-called 'unstructured cores'.

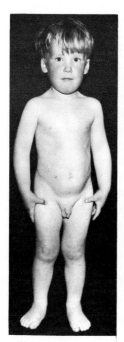
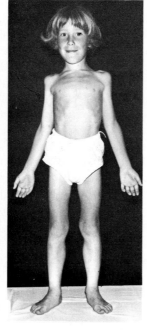

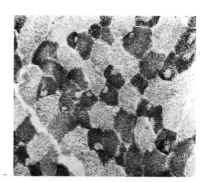

Fig. 4.2c

Fig. 4.2a   Fig. 4.2b

Fig. 4.2d

Fig. 4.2. Central core disease in a three-year-old boy *(a)* with normal motor milestones and minimal proximal muscle weakness. No progression of muscle weakness at seven years *(b)*. Initial biopsy at four years *(c)* showed normal subdivision into fibre types and only about 3 per cent of type 1 fibres affected. Recent follow-up biopsy at 16 years of age showed a dramatic change *(d)*, with undifferentiated muscle comprising entirely type 1 fibres and uniform involvement throughout by central cores, despite no apparent clinical deterioration. This biopsy was now identical in appearance to his mother's. On electron-microscopy, cores have a band structure but are out of phase with surrounding normal muscle, and also devoid of mitochondria and other subcellular elements *(e)*.

Fig. 4.2e

37

Minicore disease

Engel and colleagues (1971) documented two unrelated children with a benign, congenital, non-progressive myopathy associated with multifocal areas of degeneration in the muscle fibres (Fig. 4.3). The first case, a boy of 13, had had non-progressive weakness of the trunk and extremities all his life, with delay in attaining motor milestones. He was able to walk at 18 months but was unable to climb stairs until nine years of age. There were no other affected members in his family. The second case, an 11-year-old girl, had had non-progressive weakness from infancy. Her muscle weakness was initially ascribed to a congenital heart lesion and cardiac failure at four months, but after cardiac surgery the heart function improved but the muscle weakness did not. She walked at 22 months but could not get up again if she fell over. At seven years she still had diffuse weakness, affecting the upper limbs more than lower and proximal muscles more than distal, and also had associated ptosis, scoliosis and contractures at the tendo calcaneus and elbow flexors.

Most subsequent case reports suggest a very mild condition, usually presenting later in childhood rather than with severe hypotonia in early infancy. The recordings of affected twin males (Heffner *et al.* 1967) and of three affected siblings in one family with unaffected parents who were first cousins (Dubowitz 1978) suggest an autosomal recessive pattern of inheritance.

It thus appears that minicore disease is probably distinct from central core disease, both structurally and genetically.

Nemaline myopathy ('rod body' myopathy)

Shy *et al.* (1963) described 'nemaline myopathy, a new congenital myopathy' in a four-year-old girl who had been a floppy infant and had muscle weakness affecting her upper limbs more than the lower. They suggested the name 'nemaline myopathy' from the Greek *nema* (thread) because they were uncertain whether these rod-like structures were individual rods or an undulating thread-like structure. Conen *et al.* (1963) independently observed 'myogranules' in the biopsy of a very similar four-year-old boy with hypotonia and non-progressive weakness.

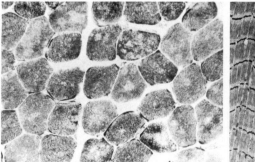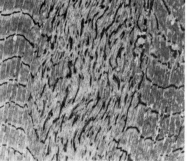

Fig. 4.3. Minicore disease: multiple small cores in muscle biopsy from 10-year-old boy with mild, non-progressive form of weakness (*left:* NADH-TR reaction × 255). Electronmicroscopy *(right)* shows the minicores to be circumscribed oval structures, not running the length of the muscle fibres as in central core disease, and showing marked disruption of normal band pattern.

Clinical features

Nemaline myopathy is probably one of the most common congenital myopathies and there have been several subsequent reports. While many cases have been relatively mild and non-progressive, and indeed one of the cases reported by Gonatas *et al.* (1966) was a symptom-free sibling of the index case, others have been more severe and even fatal (Engel 1967, Shafiq *et al.* 1967). On clinical examination many cases have had reduced muscle bulk, and it is of particular interest that the cases of Krabbe's 'universal muscular atrophy' (a diagnosis that will be familiar to an earlier generation of paediatricians) included by Ford (1960) in the earlier edition of his textbook of paediatric neurology were subsequently shown to have nemaline myopathy (Hopkins *et al.* 1966). By coincidence, the case described by Conen *et al.* (1963) had also previously been labelled as Krabbe's disease on clinical grounds, underlining again the limitations of non-specific diagnostic labels in relation to the congenital myopathies.

Many reported cases have had associated skeletal dysmorphism, with kyphoscoliosis, pigeon chest, pes cavus, high-arched palate and an unusually long face (Conen *et al.* 1963, Engel *et al.* 1964, Price *et al.* 1965, Spiro *et al.* 1966, Hudgson *et al.* 1967). However, this dysmorphism is not unique to nemaline myopathy; it is also observed in some other congenital myopathies (see, for example, myotubular myopathy below).

Kuitonnen *et al.* (1972) drew attention to the high incidence of respiratory problems which occurred in three of their four cases, and which also seemed to be a consistent feature of early-onset cases previously recorded in the literature. This has also been our own experience in a number of cases.

Clinical severity is very variable; some cases present in late childhood with mild weakness and in retrospect may have had a history of delayed motor milestones, whereas others may present in early infancy with hypotonia and associated weakness (Figs. 4.4, 4.5), and may die early of respiratory failure.

Inheritance

The familial nature of the disease was established by Spiro and Kennedy (1965) in their study of an affected mother and daughter, and the two siblings reported by Gonatas *et al.* (1966) turned out to be cousins of Spiro and Kennedy's index case. Hopkins *et al.* (1966) also documented an affected mother and daughter. These affected families conform to a dominant inheritance pattern, with variable clinical expression. On the other hand, muscle biopsy was completely normal in both parents of the fatal case I had the opportunity of studying (Shafiq *et al.* 1967), in the two cases of Kuitonnen *et al.* (1972) and in the families of two subsequent isolated cases (Dubowitz 1978). There have also been numerous other reports of sporadic cases (Conen *et al.* 1963, Engel *et al.* 1964, Price *et al.* 1965, Hudgson *et al.* 1967).

Histopathology

The rods are easily overlooked on routine haematoxylin and eosin staining but are readily demonstrated with the Gomori trichrome stain, particularly in adequately prepared cryostat sections; they are a striking red colour in contrast to the blue-green

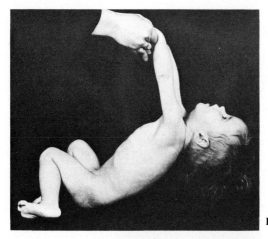

Fig. 4.4a

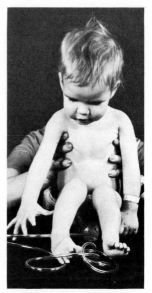

Fig. 4.4b

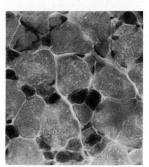

Fig. 4.4d

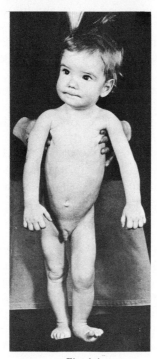

Fig. 4.4c

Fig. 4.4. Nemaline myopathy in a nine-month-old infant who had had a normal neonatal period but who developed hypotonia and subsequent weakness from two months of age. He had poor head control *(a)*, was unable to sit unsupported *(b)*, but was able to stand with support *(c)*. Needle biopsy from the quadriceps showed the typical rod structures on trichrome stain *(d)* and complete disruption of muscle architecture; numerous electron dense rods in these fibres were seen on electron-microscopy *(e)*. He died suddenly at 18 months, following a mild respiratory infection. Biopsy of both parents was normal.

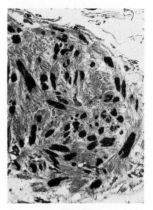

Fig. 4.4e

of the muscle fibres (Fig. 4.4).

There is often a disparity in the size of the muscle fibres, with one population of large fibres, often strikingly hypertrophied, and another of very atrophic fibres. The rods seem to occur particularly in the atrophic fibres.

On electronmicroscopy the rods are readily demonstrable as dense structures, often of rectangular shape, with a lattice-like pattern of consistent periodicity, and apparently arising in continuity with the Z lines (Fig. 4.4). They are thought to be an abnormal deposition of Z band protein, and recent advances in immunocytochemical techniques should help to identify the exact nature of the rods.

Although doubt has been expressed as to the specificity of these rod structures, since they may occur in association with numerous other pathological conditions in muscle, it does seem that there is an entity of nemaline myopathy as a congenital myopathy.

Myotubular myopathy

In 1966, Spiro and colleagues suggested the name 'myotubular myopathy' for the histological changes observed in the biopsies from a 12-year-old boy, because of the striking resemblance to the myotubes of fetal muscle. The clinical history was somewhat complex. The child had had delay in early motor milestones and at three months was still unable to raise his head in the prone position. Bilateral subdural haematomas were evacuated surgically at six months. Although he walked by 17 months, he was never able to run. From the age of five years he also developed convulsions. There was generalized weakness, which appeared to be progressive, and associated ptosis, external ophthalmoplegia and facial diplegia. On biopsy of the gastrocnemius, the muscle fibres were normal in size, but in about 85 per cent of

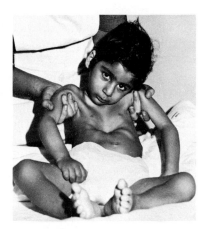

Fig. 4.5. Nemaline myopathy in a three-year-old boy with marked hypotonia and weakness from birth, and recurrent respiratory infections. (Note the pectus excavatum.) He was unable to sit or stand unaided and subsequently died of pneumonia at 3½ years.

41

them there were one to four centrally placed nuclei, surrounded by an area devoid of myofibrils. Similar changes were noted in about 45 per cent of fibres in a second biopsy. Spiro and colleagues considered these abnormal fibres to be comparable to the myotubes of developing muscle and postulated an arrest in the development of the muscle at cellular level.

Sher *et al.* (1967) subsequently observed similar pathological changes in the muscle of two Negro sisters, aged 18 and 16 years, and their symptom-free mother. The first sister had delay in early motor milestones, generalized atrophy of the musculature, a slowly progressive weakness of the skeletal muscles, ptosis, external ophthalmoplegia and facial weakness. The clinical photograph, with the long, thin face, shows a striking resemblance to the case of Spiro *et al.* (1966) and also to the 'dysmorphic' features of some reported cases of nemaline myopathy. The younger sister, who had not been floppy as an infant and had no delay in motor milestones, showed a fairly diffuse wasting and weakness of the limbs and bilateral ptosis, but no facial weakness or ophthalmoplegia. Biopsy of the rectus femoris and gastrocnemius in both sisters showed central nuclei in the majority of fibres. In the mother's gastrocnemius, about a third of the fibres had internal nuclei.

Because Sher and colleagues were not convinced of the pathogenesis of the condition, they suggested an alternative descriptive title of 'centronuclear myopathy' rather than myotubular. However, the term 'myotubular myopathy' seems to have become firmly entrenched and will probably survive in spite of the possibly false premises for its choice.

Since the initial reports a number of further cases have been documented, with variability both in clinical manifestation and in muscle morphology.

Clinical picture

In general the clinical picture in these patients has been one of varying degrees of weakness, often including ptosis and weakness of the external ocular muscles, as well as weakness of the axial musculature (Fig. 4.6) (Bethlem *et al.* 1968, Kinoshita and Cadman 1968, Badurska *et al.* 1969, Campbell *et al.* 1969, Munsat *et al.* 1969, van Wijngaarden *et al.* 1969, Vital *et al.* 1970, Ortiz de Zarate and Maruffo 1970). Although most of these cases had had symptoms of weakness from infancy, occasionally the disease did not present symptomatically until later in childhood, and in some the extra-ocular weakness was not prominent. The disease seemed to be either non-progressive or only slowly progressive in most cases. One child, who also had convulsions or apnoeic spells, died at eight years of age. The majority of recorded cases have been children under 10 years of age, but at least three adults have been reported (Bethlem *et al.* 1968, Karpati *et al.* 1970, Vital *et al.* 1970).

Genetics

It would appear from the number of instances already recorded of multiple cases within a family that the condition is certainly genetically determined. Although Sher *et al.* (1967) suggested an autosomal recessive inheritance for their two affected female cases and the clinically normal but affected mother, an alternative explanation would be an autosomal dominant gene with variable clinical severity. This mode of

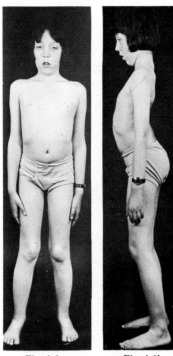

Fig. 4.6c

Fig. 4.6a   Fig. 4.6b

Fig. 4.6. Myotubular myopathy in 14-year-old boy with hypotonia from birth, feeding difficulties in the newborn period requiring tube feeding for three weeks, and delay in motor milestones. He sat at 14 months, stood at 16 months and walked at 18 months. His weakness was fairly static over the years, but he developed marked lordosis of the whole dorsolumbar spine. There was associated ptosis, facial weakness and external ophthalmoplegia (*a* and *b*). Muscle biopsy showed large central nuclei in most fibres (c).

inheritance would also be compatible with the familial cases of Munsat *et al.* (1969) and Ortiz de Zarate and Maruffo (1970). As in other dominantly inherited conditions, it is important to do muscle biopsies to look for subclinical affected cases, as in the case of Sher *et al.* (1967).

Myotubular myopathy with type 1 fibre hypotrophy

In another—and possibly related—condition, central nuclei occur in fibres which are also reduced in diameter and are selectively of the histochemical type 1 fibres. Engel *et al.* (1968) first recorded an 11-month-old boy with a severe and progressive weakness of the limbs and respiratory muscles but no ocular or facial weakness. The child died at 18 months, and at autopsy there was no abnormality in the nervous system. Although agreeing that the small fibres in their patient did have some resemblance to embryonic myotubes, Engel *et al.* were not convinced that these were true myotubes or that they had any unique significance in this child's disease. They attached more importance to the histochemical pattern and suggested calling it 'type 1 fibre hypotrophy with central nuclei', implying a maturational arrest rather than an atrophy of type 1 fibres. Further cases with this pathological picture (Bethlem *et al.* 1968, Karpati *et al.* 1970) have suggested that the entity is clinically different from the typical motubular myopathy, and also that it is not necessarily a progressive and fatal disease as was the first case reported by Engel and colleagues (1968). Clinical and pathological features of this condition are illustrated in Figure 4.7.

43

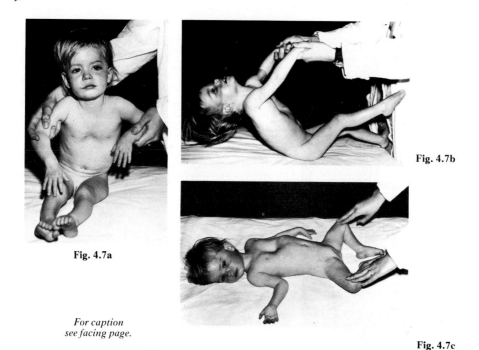

Fig. 4.7b

Fig. 4.7a

For caption
see facing page.

Fig. 4.7c

Severe X-linked myotubular myopathy

A severe form of myotubular myopathy was described by van Wijngaarden *et al.*
(1969) in a Dutch family with an apparent x-linked pattern of inheritance and a 25
per cent mortality of affected males (two out of eight) in the neonatal period. Two of
the clinically healthy female carriers also had myotubes in their muscle biopsies.
Barth *et al.* (1975) subsequently documented another large Dutch family, unrelated
to the previous one, which also had an x-linked pattern of inheritance. There was 100
per cent mortality of affected males (13 out of 13) in the early newborn period as a
result of associated respiratory insufficiency. In some there was also a history of
diminished fetal movements *in utero* or of hydramnios. Muscle biopsies from five
clinically normal female carriers showed mild pathological changes and myotubes
were present in four of them.

I have recently had the opportunity of investigating such a child who survived the
neonatal period and numerous respiratory problems, due mainly to the intensive
management of his devoted parents, and who subsequently showed some improvement in motor function (Fig. 4.8).

Nomenclature

Although the controversy as to the nature and pathogenesis of the 'myotubes' in
myotubular myopathy will probably continue, as will the question of identity or
overlap between the cases with and without type 1 hypotrophy, it seems that the
histological and histochemical features do have a consistent pattern. In addition to
the unusually large, centrally-placed nuclei, the ATPase reaction (which normally

44

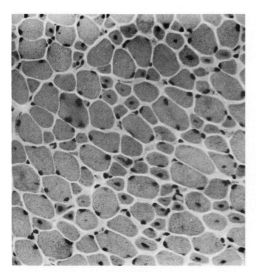

Fig. 4.7d

Fig. 4.7. Myotubular myopathy with type 1 fibre hypotrophy. 18-month-old infant with hypotonia from birth and delay in motor milestones. Unable to sit unsupported *(a)* and still with marked head lag *(b)*. She also had mild facial weakness, ptosis and external ophthalmoplegia. There was marked pectus excavatum *(c)* and she suffered recurrent respiratory infections. Muscle biopsy *(d)* showed a mixture of small and large fibres and frequent central nuclei, especially in the small fibres, which were histochemically mainly type 1. She subsequently did remarkably well, walked at 2½ years, became less prone to chest infections, and the pectus excavatum seemed to fill out. The ptosis, facial weakness and external ophthalmoplegia persisted (*e, f,* aged 6½ years; *g,* aged 7½ years). Her chest became very thin and flat anteroposteriorly, with very small lung volume and reserve capacity. Following a respiratory infection she went into respiratory failure at the age of nine years, needing intubation and mechanical ventilation. After a stormy course she recovered, returning to her previous status. (Compare posture of patient in Fig. 4.6.)

(Fig. 4.7e-g)

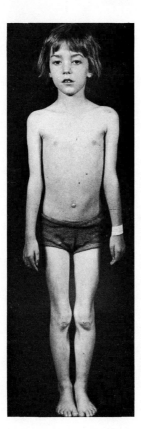

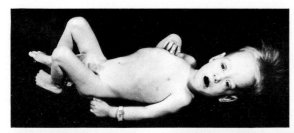

Fig. 4.8a

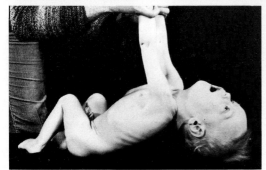

Fig. 4.8b

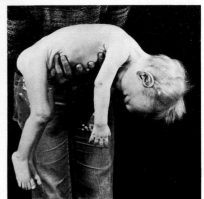

Fig. 4.8c

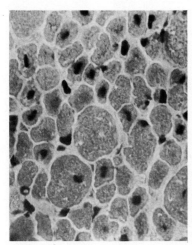

Fig. 4.8d

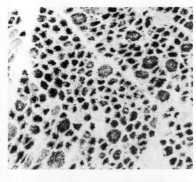

Fig. 4.8e

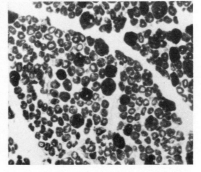

Fig. 4.8f

For caption see facing page.

46

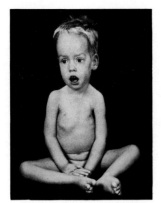

Fig. 4.8g

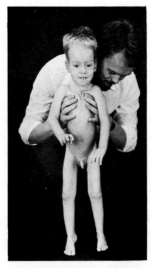
Fig. 4.8h

Fig. 4.8. Severe X-linked myotubular myopathy. Nine-month-old infant who had asphyxia and severe respiratory problems at birth, followed by hypoglycemia: initially diagnosed as hypotonic cerebral palsy. When assessed at nine months *(a-c)* he still had severe respiratory deficit, marked flattening and poor movement of the left chest. His skeletal muscle weakness was disproportionate to his hypotonia; in addition to poor head control he also had mild facial weakness, ptosis and external ophthalmoplegia. Clinical diagnosis of severe myotubular myopathy was confirmed by needle biopsy, showing a large number of fibres with central nuclei *(d)*, with aggregation of oxidative enzyme stain in the centre of fibres *(e)* but clear central zones ('holes') with ATPase reaction *(f)*. He was the first child of unrelated parents, and family history was negative. Needle biopsy of symptom-free mother showed focal abnormalities in the muscle, confirming an X-linked inheritance, and subsequently similar changes were found in her symptom-free sister. The child required regular pharyngeal suction. Apart from several life-threatening respiratory infections his general condition steadily improved and his limbs increased in strength. A year later he was able to sit unsupported and had much better head control *(g, h)*.

shows up the myofibrils of the muscle fibre) shows a clear area in the centre of the fibre (looking like a hole) at the site of the internal nuclei. In contrast, the oxidative enzyme reaction shows an aggregation of stain in the centre, often with a halo around it. This oxidative enzyme picture is not seen in normal myotubes of fetal muscle and seems to be quite distinctive for myotubular myopathy (Fig. 4.8).

Mixed myopathies

Despite the relative rarity of these individual congenital myopathies and the controversy as to the specificity of the various structural changes, a number of instances have been recorded of multiple pathological patterns within the same biopsy.

Co-existence of nemaline myopathy and cores in the same patient

Since the rods in nemaline myopathy appear to arise from the Z line and streaming of the Z line is a common feature in the cores of central core disease, it is perhaps not surprising that an overlap of the conditions has been observed. The presence of both central cores and rods in the same muscle was observed in one case by Afifi *et al.* (1965), who speculated that the two conditions might have a similar

47

pathogenesis. Karpati *et al.* (1971) observed cores in the diaphragm of a fatal case of nemaline myopathy.

One of the infants I have investigated with severe hypotonia and weakness showed the coexistence of nemaline myopathy with minicores.

Co-existence of minicores with whorled fibres

Two siblings presenting with hypotonia from birth, initial feeding difficulty in the newborn period, and delay in attaining motor milestones have shown a strikingly similar histological picture of minicores in association with whorled fibres (Fig. 4.9). Whorled fibres are commonly seen in chronic dystrophies, and also in chronic neuropathies where presumably they are related to a reinnervation process. On electronmicroscopy the muscle fibres showed some elongated, unstructured cores

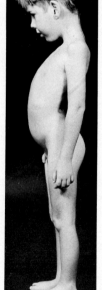

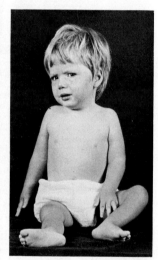

Fig. 4.9c

Fig. 4.9a

Fig. 4.9b

For caption see facing page.

Fig. 4.9d

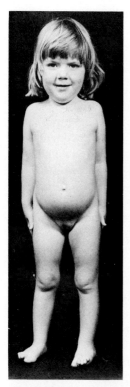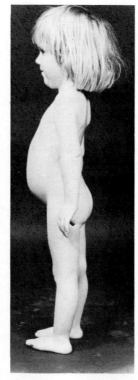

Fig. 4.9e *(left)*, **4.9f** *(right)*

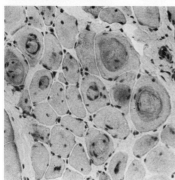

Fig. 4.9g

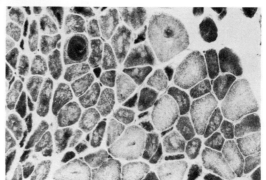

Fig. 4.9h

Fig. 4.9. Whorled fibre myopathy with minicores. Five-year-old boy *(a, b)* with hypotonia from birth and delay in motor milestones. Stood at 14 months, walked at 21 months with gradual improvement, becoming more steady on his legs, but still had difficulty getting up from the floor. Able to ascend steps one at a time. No weakness of facial or ocular muscles. His younger sister had a similar history of hypotonia from birth, with delayed motor milestones and also initial feeding difficulty in the newborn period. She sat unsupported at nine months but was still unable to walk unaided when first assessed at two years *(c, d)*. She walked well with one hand held and in the ensuing few months began to take a few steps unaided, and subsequently walked well without support *(e, f,* aged 3½ years). Like her brother, she had marked lumbar lordosis but no facial or external ocular weakness or ptosis. EMGs in both children showed a myopathic pattern, and needle biopsy a striking pattern of whorled fibres and minicores on histological and histochemical analysis *(g, h)*. Electronmicroscopy showed circumscribed minicores, but also some unstructured cores running the length of the fibre.

running the length of the fibre, as well as typical circumscribed minicores. On follow-up the children showed no apparent increase in weakness; if anything, there was improvement in muscle strength and function.

Congenital fibre type disproportion

This condition was initially recognized by Brooke (1973), purely on the basis of a consistent histochemical pattern in some of the childhood muscle biopsies he was reviewing. The type 1 fibres were smaller than the type 2 fibres by a margin of more than 12 per cent of the diameter of the type 2 fibres (Fig. 4.10), in contrast to normal muscle in children, in which type 1 and type 2 fibres were of approximately equal size. Brooke then recognized a fairly consistent clinical picture in these cases. All the children were floppy infants, the condition being noted at or shortly after birth. In half of the cases contractures of various muscles of either the hands or feet had been noted. One patient had torticollis due to a contracted sternomastoid. Half of the patients also had congenital dislocation of the hip, either bilaterally or unilaterally. The degree of weakness varied quite considerably: it seemed to involve all the muscles of the trunk and extremities, although in some patients the legs appeared to be more involved than the arms. It was so severe in one patient that little voluntary movement of the arms or legs had been possible until almost two years of age. In other cases the weakness was mild enough to cause only a delay in the development of the motor milestones, rather than any obvious paralysis. In some there appeared to have been an initial progression of the weakness during the first year of life, but in no case did Brooke see any progression once the child had attained two years of age. As the child grew older, the disease became static or improvement took place.

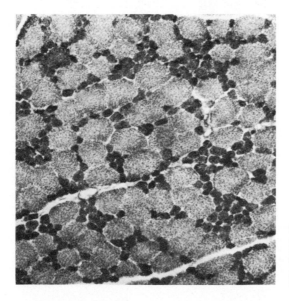

Fig. 4.10. Congenital fibre type disproportion. Muscle biopsy from four-year-old female reported by Lenard and Goebel (1975), showing small type 1 fibres (dark staining) in contrast to normal-sized type 2 fibres (NADH-TR × 150).

Recurrent respiratory infections were frequently a problem during the first year of life. There was an associated abnormality in stature: height was below the 10th percentile in eight of the 14 patients, and 12 were below the 3rd percentile in weight, even though the birthweight had been normal in most cases. Eight patients had a high-arched palate, and a kyphoscoliosis was seen in six children as they grew older. Deformities of the feet were common, including either flat feet or, occasionally, high-arched feet.

About half of Brooke's patients had a relative with a similar clinical condition, mostly affected siblings, which suggested an autosomal recessive pattern of inheritance. However, one patient had an affected father and brother, suggesting a dominant mechanism.

The condition may be difficult to distinguish initially from the early stages of Werdnig-Hoffmann's disease, when the classical picture of pathological change may not yet have developed (Dubowitz 1978). In early cases of severe spinal muscular atrophy one may find universally small fibres, but with the type 1 fibres being significantly smaller than the type 2 fibres. One should always be guided by the clinical picture, and a classical case of spinal muscular atrophy with the typical clinical features of proximal weakness affecting the legs more than the arms, with associated trunk and intercostal weakness, but sparing the face, should be diagnosed as such even in the presence of an atypical biopsy picture. There is also clinical overlap of congenital fibre type disproportion with congenital myotonic dystrophy, which histologically also shows a selective atrophy of type 1 fibres (see below).

Fardeau et al. (1975) studied two sisters with neonatal hypotonia and congenital fibre type disproportion. Type 1 fibres were at the lower limit of normal size and type 2 fibres were larger than normal. No abnormality was found on electronmicroscopy. The father's biopsy also showed small type 1 fibres, with a bimodal distribution. These authors considered that the small size of type 1 fibres was more likely to be due to a lack of development rather than to atrophy, but the mechanism of this hypotrophy remains unknown.

It is possible that the condition is not a uniformly benign one, since Lenard and Goebel (1975) documented a case with fairly severe weakness and associated respiratory deficit necessitating tracheostomy.

In a review of eight cases with possible fibre type disproportion, Cavanagh et al. (1979) commented on the variable clinical picture, and in one of their cases who died the histological picture of the muscle at autopsy was indistinguishable from a congenital muscular dystrophy. The original biopsy from this patient had been interpreted as fibre type disproportion, and this case illustrates the difficulty in distinguishing the picture from the variable fibre size which is a feature of early or mild myopathies, and which I have suggested calling 'minimal change myopathy' (Dubowitz 1978). In addition, their unusual case also had elevated creatine phosphokinase, which would support a diagnosis of congenital dystrophy rather than fibre type disproportion.

It thus seems likely that the histological picture of fibre type disproportion may well reflect a mixed bag of entities and the diagnosis should probably be very strictly reserved for those cases with no other histological change but a striking disproportion in size of the different fibre types, the type 1 fibres being smaller than normal, and the type 2 normal-sized or enlarged.

The two siblings with non-progressive congenital myopathy who I described in the first edition of *The Floppy Infant* (Dubowitz 1969, p. 34), with gradually improving hypotonia and weakness and whose biopsies showed selective reduction in the size of type 1 fibres, probably conform to this histochemical diagnosis and also resemble other cases clinically. A further case followed from birth into childhood is illustrated in Fig. 4.11.

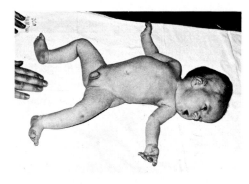

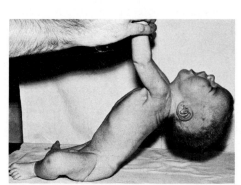

Fig. 4.11. Congenital fibre type disproportion. Infant's mother was concerned about diminished movements *in utero*. He was delivered by elective caesarean section because of transverse lie (and a previous caesarean section), and was extremely hypotonic and immobile at birth, with parietal cephalhaematoma (rare in non-vaginal deliveries). He was tube fed for two months because of sucking and swallowing difficulties and also had mild facial weakness. At four weeks he was still very hypotonic, with marked head lag *(a, b)*. Muscle biopsy of quadriceps showed variability in fibre size, type 1 fibres being mainly smaller than type 2 *(c)*, and the diagnosis of congenital fibre type disproportion was made. (However, this biopsy picture is very similar to that seen in the pre-pathological phase of infantile spinal muscular atrophy.) The child steadily improved, and by 14 months was sitting with support and taking some weight on his legs *(d, e)*; from two years he was able to walk unaided, after which he developed a slowly progressive scoliosis *(f, g,* aged four years). CPK (28 iu/l) and EMG were normal. Follow-up biopsy has not yet been done.

Fig. 4.11a *(upper)*, **4.11b** *(lower)*

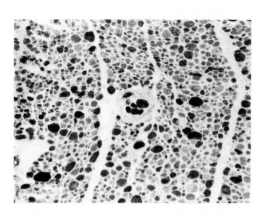

Fig. 4.11c

52

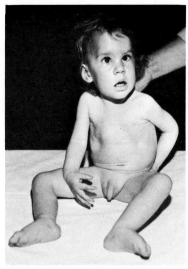

Fig. 4.11d

For caption see facing page.

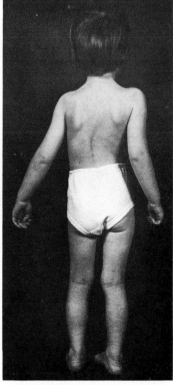

Fig. 4.11e

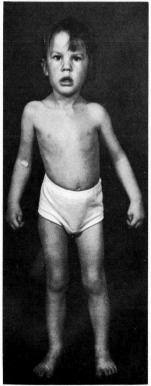

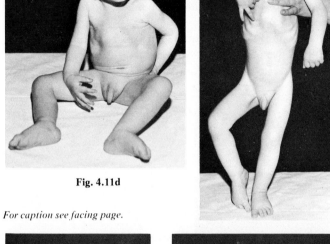

Fig. 4.11f *(left)*,
4.11g *(right)*

Congenital type 1 fibre predominance

Brooke (1977) has drawn attention to another histochemical entity, namely a striking predominance of type 1 fibres (more than 60 per cent of the total number of fibres in a biopsy specimen) as the only abnormal feature in children presenting with congenital hypotonia and delay in reaching motor milestones. Some cases have had associated skeletal anomalies, such as flat feet or pes cavus, congenital hip dislocation and, on rare occasions, kyphoscoliosis. The condition appears to be benign, with a tendency to improvement.

A similar observation has been made in a number of isolated floppy infants I have seen and also in two siblings presenting with hypotonia and delayed milestones, suggesting an autosomal recessive pattern of inheritance (Fig. 4.12).

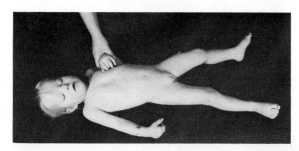

Fig. 4.12a

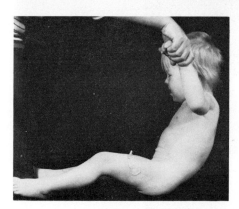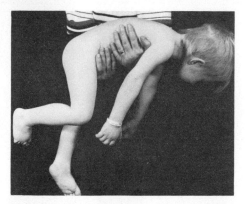

Fig. 4.12b *(left)*, 4.12c *(right)*. For captions see facing page.

Mitochondrial myopathies

Mitochondrial myopathy is not a single entity, but abnormal mitochondria are a feature of a large number of different syndromes. It is also quite likely that the structural abnormalities observed in the mitochondria merely reflect an underlying metabolic abnormality, which to date is largely unidentified in most of the cases reported. Mitochondrial myopathies are likely to be missed on routine histological stains of muscle but are suspected from the presence of disrupted, red-staining fibres

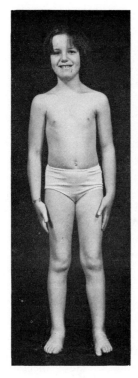

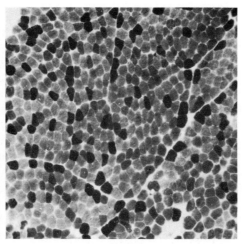

Fig. 4.12. Type 1 fibre predominance. 2½-year-old child with hypotonia from birth and delay in motor milestones. Still unable to sit up from supine or to stand or walk *(a, b)*, and poor head, trunk and limb posture in ventral suspension *(c)*. Her older sister walked at four years, and at nine years *(d)* showed fairly normal motor function. Needle biopsy from both children showed predominance of type 1 fibres but no other histological or histochemical abnormality *(e)*.

on the Gomori trichrome stain (the so-called 'ragged-red fibres') and from the presence of abnormal-looking, usually intensely-staining fibres with histochemical oxidative enzyme reactions. They are confirmed by identifying the abnormal mitochondria by electronmicroscopy.

Clinical syndromes

Mitochondrial abnormalities in the muscle were first observed in an adult patient with a hypermetabolic disorder of non-thyroid origin (Luft *et al.* 1962). This is a very rare entity and it was almost 10 years before a second case was identified (Haydar *et al.* 1971). Meanwhile, an extensive literature grew on mitochondrial abnormalities in association with a wide range of neuromuscular disorders, but without hypermetabolism.

Mitochondrial abnormalities in the muscle are a consistent feature of the so-called oculocraniosomatic syndrome (Olson *et al.* 1972) ('opthalmoplegia plus', Drachmann 1968; Kearns-Sayre's syndrome, Kearns and Sayre 1958), which is characterized by a combination of pigmentary retinopathy, external ophthalmoplegia and heart block; in addition, there is a wide range of associated features, including growth retardation, intellectual impairment, ataxia, deafness and other features (for review see Dubowitz 1978). The condition usually presents in later childhood with an associated mild proximal girdle weakness.

Hackett *et al.* (1973) studied two sisters with severe muscle weakness, nerve deafness and growth failure. There was marked excretion of alanine in the urine, and also hyperalaninaemia and reduced clearance from the blood of oral alanine load. There was raised blood pyruvate and also lactic acidaemia. One child had a fatal episode of lactic acidosis. Her cardiac muscle also showed morphological mitochondrial abnormalities.

Subsequently Sengers *et al.* (1975) observed congenital cataracts and cardiomyopathy in seven of 22 children from three unrelated families; they found abnormal mitochondria as well as lipid and glycogen storage in both cardiac and skeletal muscle. Performance of submaximal exercise for 60 minutes led to metabolic acidosis with lactic acidaemia.

It is now well recognized that abnormal mitochondria are a common accompaniment of the lipid storage myopathies associated with carnitine deficiency (see below). In addition to the overt muscle syndromes, abnormal mitochondria have been reported in muscle biopsies taken from patients with central nervous system disorders such as Leigh's disease (Crosby and Chou 1974) and Menkes' syndrome (trichopoliodystrophy; 'kinky hair' syndrome) (French *et al.* 1972).

Biochemical abnormalities

It seems feasible that the mitochondrial abnormalities in all these disorders should be a reflection of some underlying abnormality of oxidative metabolism. Studies of mitochondrial function have shown loosely coupled oxidative phosphorylation in several cases, and there have also been suggestions of more specific abnormalities, related particularly to the cytochromes and other components of the respiratory chain.

Mitochondrial-lipid-glycogen storage myopathy

Jerusalem *et al.* (1973*b*) investigated a seven-week-old infant with profound weakness of all but the ocular muscles, combined with macroglossia and hepatomegaly. Muscle biopsies showed a marked excess of mitochondria and lipid and a mild excess of glycogen, so the authors suggested calling it mitochondria-lipid-glycogen disease of muscle. Their patient subsequently improved, and at 22 months the pathological changes in the muscle were less marked. Glycolytic enzyme levels and oxidation of labelled oleic acid and Krebs cycle intermediates were normal. A similar case documented by Di Donato *et al.* (1978) also had an associated increase in blood lactate and pyruvate and a reduction in muscle carnitine.

Three children with a mitochondrial myopathy in the muscle presented with hypotonia and weakness, usually coming on in the second year of life, and a similar over-all clinical course and picture (Figs. 4.13-4.15). Two of them resembled the syndrome of mitochondiral-lipid-glycogen disease. We are currently investigating a 5-week-old infant with severe weakness and hypotonia of the limbs and trunk and associated swallowing and breathing difficulties from birth (resembling Werdnig-Hoffmann's disease), whose muscle biopsy looks identical to the cases illustrated in Figures 4.14 and 4.15. In addition, a deficiency of cytochrome oxidase has been demonstrated both histochemically and biochemically.

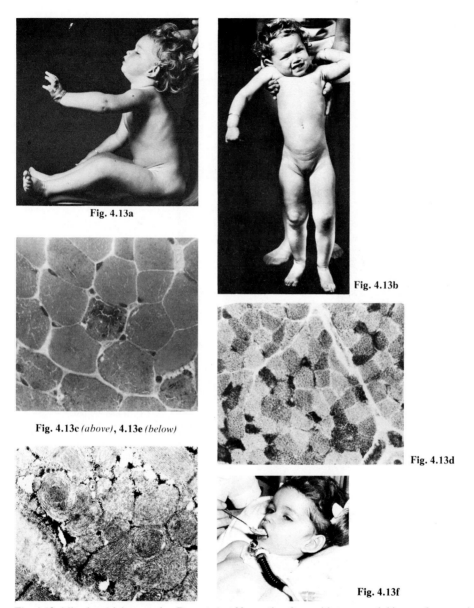

Fig. 4.13a

Fig. 4.13b

Fig. 4.13c *(above)*, 4.13e *(below)*

Fig. 4.13d

Fig. 4.13f

Fig. 4.13. Mitochondrial myopathy. Presented at 22 months of age with two-month history of progressive hypotonia, poor head control and inability to walk *(a, b)*. She subsequently showed steady deterioration, being unable to sit unaided 6 months later. CPK was initially elevated (200 iu/l) but subsequently consistently normal (80, 100 iu/l). EMG was normal. Transitory elevation of serum pyruvate and lactate, ascribed to poor dietary intake and associated ketosis. Muscle biopsy showed 'ragged red' fibres on trichrome stain *(c)* and focal, intensely staining and granular fibres on oxidative enzyme reaction in otherwise normal-looking two-fibre pattern muscle *(d)*. Grossly enlarged and distorted mitochondria were confirmed by electronmicroscopy *(e)*. There was no associated lipid or glycogen storage. At 2½ years she had respiratory failure, needing tracheostomy and mechanical ventilation *(f)*. She remained dependent on the ventilator but was mobilised in a wheelchair and mobile ventilator. She died suddenly about a year later following mechanical failure of the machine. The parents are first cousins. One sibling, born prematurely, died in the newborn period of respiratory distress syndrome.

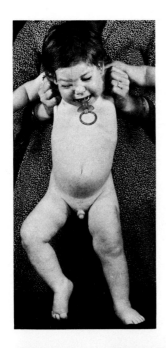
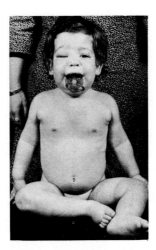

Figs. 4.14a *(left)*, **4.14b** *(above)*, **4.14c** *(below left)*, **4.14d** *(below right)*, **4.14e** *(bottom left)*, **4.14f** *(bottom right)*. For caption see facing page.

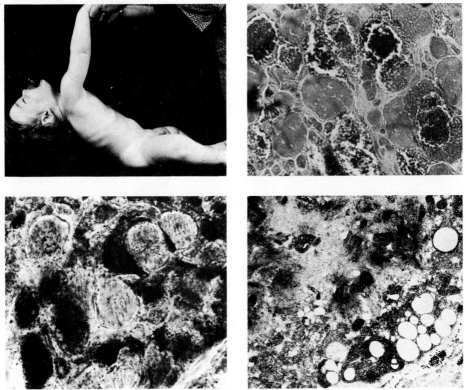

Fig. 4.14. Mitochondrial-lipid-glycogen myopathy. This 21-month-old boy had normal motor milestones and walked at 13 months. (A right ptosis from birth was ascribed to haemangioma of the eyelid.) From 14 months he developed progressive hypotonia, with unsteadiness of gait and poor head control, and lost the ability to walk by 19 months and to stand unsupported two weeks later *(a, b, c)*. CPK was elevated (240 iu/l) and EMG showed a myopathic pattern. Two previous biopsies (taken under general anaesthesia and fixed in formalin) were reported as 'myositis'. Needle biopsy from his quadriceps showed disrupted architecture, with almost universal disruption of fibres, and a striking 'ragged red' fibre appearance on trichrome stain *(d)*. There was markedly increased oxidative enzyme activity *(e)*, also glycogen and lipid. Electronmicroscopy confirmed disintegration of fibre pattern, strikingly abnormal mitochondria and presence of excess lipid and glycogen *(f)*. He subsequently remained fairly static, with some possible improvement in muscle function, on diet high in carbohydrate and low in fat, but died suddenly following gastro-intestinal upset and marked increase in weakness. A sibling born subsequently had transitory respiratory distress in the newborn period (although not premature) but thrived normally until onset of similar symptoms to his brother and confirmation of same muscle disorder (Clinical information concerning second child, courtesy of Dr. M. Jaffe, Haifa).

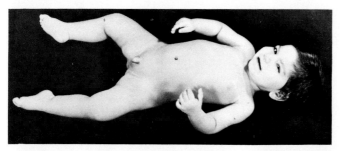

Fig. 4.15a

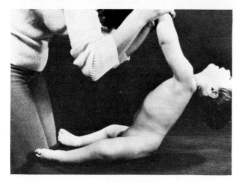

Fig. 4.15b

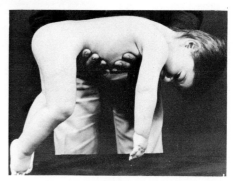

Fig. 4.15c

Fig. 4.15. Mitochondrial-lipid-glycogen storage myopathy. This child developed normally until 12 months, when he was already taking some independent steps, but then developed an illness with recurrent fevers, irritability, cough and vomiting, and associated weakness of legs and loss of ability to walk. At 17 months there was rapid deterioration in power and generalized weakness, with minimal arm or leg movement, weak voice and inability to chew or swallow. Spontaneous improvement followed and by 18 months he was again able to sit unsupported but not able to crawl or walk. When first assessed at 21 months his functional ability had remained unchanged *(a, b, c, d)* and he was still unable to stand or to roll over when lying, or to raise hands to mouth. There was associated respiratory and bulbar weakness. Weakness of limbs was more marked proximally than distally. CPK was 635 iu/l (normal <125); EMG showed myopathic change; nerve conduction velocity normal. Fasting lactate raised (3.2 mmol/l), pyruvate normal (0.09 mmol/l). Lactate:pyruvate ratio raised. Needle biopsy of quadriceps showed grossly abnormal muscle with marked loss of muscle tissue and extensive degenerative changes and 'ragged red' appearance in many fibres on trichrome stain *(e)*. There was marked excess of lipid on oil red O stain *(f)* and also excess of oxidative enzyme activity, suggesting mitochondrial abnormality *(g)*. Electronmicroscopy showed markedly disorganised muscle with excessive lipid and mitochondria, also mild excess of glycogen. Muscle carnitine was markedly reduced (7.4 nmol/mg NCP; N= 12.5 to 28), as was serum carnitine (16.5 μmol/l, N = 21 to 53 μmol/l). He was treated with D-L carnitine, initially 100 mg/kg/day and subsequently raised to 400 mg/kg/day, and also prednisone, but his condition did not improve and he subsequently needed

For remaining caption and figs. see next page.

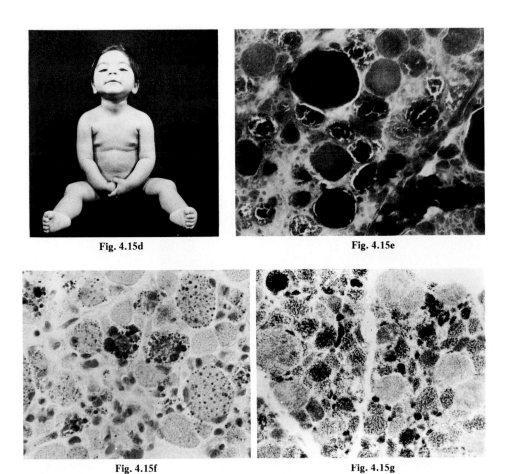

Fig. 4.15d   Fig. 4.15e

Fig. 4.15f   Fig. 4.15g

tracheostomy because of recurrent aspiration of feeds, progressive respiratory deficit and focal lung collapse. He died as a result of these respiratory complications and possibly also of cardiac involvement (there had been persistent tachycardia and mild hepatomegaly, suggesting early cardiac failure). Autopsy was refused.

Myopathies with abnormalities of other subcellular organelles

The more adequate investigation of muscle biopsies in recent times and the application of electronmicroscopy have identified abnormalities of various other subcellular organelles, apart from the mitochondria, in relation to cases of neuromuscular disorder. Many of these still involve only single case reports, so it is not yet possible to put together any consistent clinical picture. For this reason I have discussed them collectively in this section.

Reducing body myopathy

Brooke and Neville (1972) reported two infants with a progressive neuromuscular disorder from birth, who died at 2½ years and nine months respectively. The muscle showed small inclusions on light microscopy, capable of reducing tetrazolium salts histochemically, hence the suggested name. The bodies also contained RNA and glycogen and on electronmicroscopy had a distinctive appearance, being a round or oval shape and composed of densely packed, moderately osmiophilic particles, in the midst of which were non-membrane limited holes containing glycogen granules. The origin of these particles is uncertain, but they resemble inclusions found with Coxsackie virus infections.

'Fingerprint' myopathy

Engel *et al.* (1972) found abundant subsarcolemmal inclusions, consisting of complex lamellae resembling fingerprints, on electronmicroscopic examination of the muscle from a five-year-old girl with generalized weakness and hypotonia from birth; she was also mentally retarded and had a static tremor.

'Sarcotubular' myopathy

Jerusalem *et al.* (1973a) described two brothers, aged 15 and 11 years, with a congenital non-progressive myopathy, in whom the muscle showed a vacuolar myopathy on light microscopy and the presence of dilated and coalesced sarcotubular systems on electronmicroscopy.

'Zebra-body' myopathy

Lake and Wilson (1975) found rod-shaped bodies on electronmicroscopy of the muscle from a 15-year-old boy with a congenital myopathy. Light microscopy showed variation in fibre size, vacuolation, calcification and fibre splitting.

Other structures such as cytoplasmic bodies and tubular aggregates are found in association with many different myopathies and are probably not of any specific diagnostic significance.

Non-specific congenital myopathies; 'minimal change myopathy'

In some floppy infants with unequivocal muscle weakness it is not possible to pinpoint any specific pathological change in the muscle, despite fully comprehensive histochemical and electronmicroscopic investigation. In some of these biopsies the muscle looks completely normal, so presumably the cause of the weakness must reside in some functional aberration either in the nervous control of the muscle or in its biochemical functioning. In other cases evidence of minor changes in the muscle can be seen, such as variation in fibre size, but with no additional evidence of degeneration, internal nuclei, proliferation of connective tissue or other pathological change (Fig. 4.16). Similarly, electronmicroscopy occasionally shows loss of myofibrils within individual fibres but no other specific change.

For want of a better name I have used the term 'minimal change myopathy' for these latter cases. At follow-up most of these children have remained clinically unchanged, with no apparent deterioration in their muscle dysfunction. It was possible to make a further histological assessment of the muscle at the time of tenotomy of the tendo calcaneus in one of these cases, and this showed a strikingly dystrophic picture consistent with a congenital dystrophy (see Chapter 5). Thus it seems likely that the early minimal myopathy changes in some instances may reflect a congenital dystrophy with pathological progression but with no apparent clinical progression, presumably due to some compensatory functional improvement in the muscle. A similar case was reported by Cavanagh *et al.* (1979) as an unusual variant of congenital fibre type disproportion.

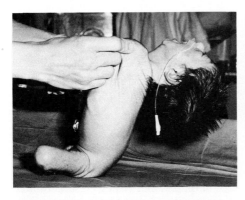

Fig. 4.16a *(left)*, 4.16b *(above)*

Fig. 4.16. 'Minimal change myopathy'. Infant born at 37 weeks gestation with marked hypotonia and gross head lag in association with 'arthrogryposis', with calcaneovalgus deformity of feet, extension deformity of hands and fixed flexion of knees *(a, b, c)*. Limbs could readily be folded back into their intra-uterine posture *(d)*. There was also marked sucking and swallowing difficulty, necessitating tube feeding, together with recurrent respiratory distress associated with aspiration. Needle biopsy showed abnormal-looking biopsy with variation in fibre size but no evidence of degeneration or denervation *(e)*. He subsequently died at two months and autopsy revealed atrophic-looking spinal cord with marked thinning of nerve roots, suggesting neurogenic lesion. A subsequent pregnancy ended in a stillbirth at 37 weeks gestation, with no postural deformities, and autopsy was refused.

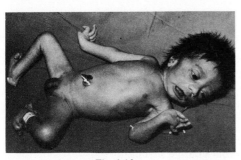

Fig. 4.16c

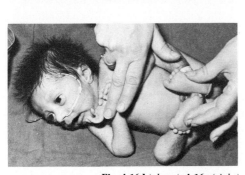

Fig. 4.16d *(above)*, 4.16e *(right)*

B. METABOLIC MYOPATHIES

One might presume that all neuromuscular disorders with a genetic basis are due to an underlying metabolic abnormality, but in the vast majority of syndromes, and in particular the muscular dystrophies, no such abnormality has yet been identified.

However, there have been a number of significant advances in recent years in the recognition of specific metabolic disorders, some confined to muscle only and others part of a more generalized disease. The majority have been related to either glycogen or lipid metabolism, but other disorders such as periodic paralysis and malignant hyperpyrexia and various syndromes associated with myoglobinuria probably also have a metabolic basis.

The mitochondrial myopathies probably belong in this group as well, but their transfer can await the more accurate definition of the underlying biochemical derangements which will surely be forthcoming in the next few years.

Glycogenoses

There is a growing list of glycogenoses with identified enzyme deficiency (Table 4.1) and at least four of these glycogenoses affect muscle:

Type II — amylo-1,4-glucosidase (acid maltase) deficiency;
Type III — amylo-1,6-glucosidase (debranching enzyme) deficiency;
Type V — myophosphorylase deficiency;
Type VII — phosphofructokinase deficiency;
and possibly also
Type IV — amylo $(1,4\rightarrow1,6)$ transglucosidase (branching enzyme) deficiency.

The most important one in the case of the floppy infant is type II (Pompe's disease), which is a generalized glycogenosis affecting skeletal muscle directly, but also affecting the anterior horn cells of the spinal cord and thus presenting with a clinical picture similar to spinal muscular atrophy. Type III is also likely to present with hypotonia or muscle weakness, whereas types V and VII characteristically present with cramps associated with exercise, and at a much later age.

Type II glycogenosis

This is the most severe form of glycogenosis and the classical form (Pompe's disease) is usually fatal in infancy (Fig. 4.17). It is a generalized disease, involving not only liver, heart and skeletal muscle, but also many other tissues such as the central nervous system and kidneys. Since the same enzyme deficiency has been demonstrated in the heart, liver and skeletal muscle (Hers 1963), the traditional 'cardiac glycogenosis' is no longer regarded as a separate entity.

Affected infants present either with severe hypotonia and weakness or with symptoms of cardiac or respiratory failure. The muscle weakness is due to direct involvement of the muscle itself or to the involvement of the anterior horn cells of the cord (or both). These severely affected infants look very similar clinically to cases of infantile spinal muscular atrophy.

There is some variability in the clinical severity of the severe type, and some cases present a little later and may show somewhat less severe involvement (Fig. 4.18).

TABLE 4.1
Glycogenoses

Type	Enzyme deficiency	Eponymous or other names	Skeletal muscle affected	Clinical features	Other tissues affected
I	Glucose-6-phosphatase	von Gierke's disease	No		
II	α-1,4-glucosidase (acid maltase)	Pompe's disease	Yes	(a) Severe form: generalized; resembles infantile spinal muscular atrophy	Heart, nervous system, kidneys, leucocytes
				(b) Mild form: resembles limb girdle dystrophy	? Heart
III	Amylo-1,6-glucosidase ('debranching enzyme')	Limit dextrinosis Forbes' disease Cori's disease	Yes	Infantile hypotonia Mild weakness	Hepatic Hypoglycaemia Ketosis Leucocytes
IV	α-1,4-glucan: α-1,4-glucan 6-glycosyl transferase ('branching enzyme'; amylo (1,4→1,6) transglucosidase	Amylopectinosis Andersen's disease	? Some cases only	Usually no muscle symptoms In some wasting or weakness	Hepatomegaly Cirrhosis Splenomegaly
V	Muscle phosphorylase	McArdle's disease	Yes	Exercise intolerance Muscle cramps Fatigue Myoglobinuria	None
VI	Liver phosphorylase		No		
VII	Phosphofructokinase	Tarui's disease	Yes	Exercise intolerance Muscle cramps Fatigue Myoglobinuria	Erythrocytes

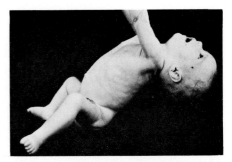

Fig. 4.17a

Fig. 4.17b

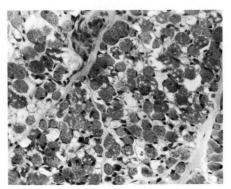

Fig. 4.17c

Fig. 4.17d

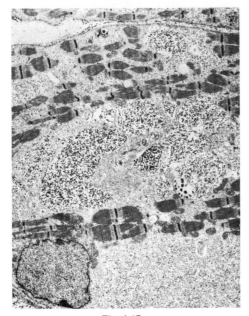

Fig. 4.17. Type II glycogenosis (Pompe's disease). Four-month-old infant with marked hypotonia from birth *(a. b)*, congenital dislocation of the hips, feeding difficulty and recurrent respiratory infection. Associated cardiomegaly and hepatomegaly. EMG showed characteristic 'pseudomyotonic' bursts and ECG giant complexes with short P-R interval. Quadriceps biopsy showed striking vacuoles in muscle fibres *(c)*, which contained PAS-positive glycogen *(d)*. Electronmicroscopy showed extensive loss of myofibrils, with increase in glycogen, some of which was membrane-bound and presumably lysosomal *(e)*. Biochemical studies confirmed diagnosis: glycogen content was 15 times normal and acid maltase was absent. She died of heart failure at eight months.

Fig. 4.17e

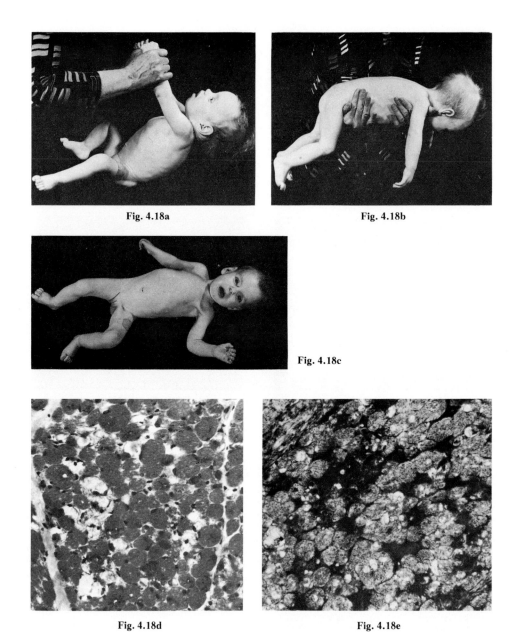

Fig. 4.18a

Fig. 4.18b

Fig. 4.18c

Fig. 4.18d

Fig. 4.18e

Fig. 4.18. Type II glycogenosis. Six-month-old girl with hypotonia and weakness from birth and with cardiomegaly and hepatomegaly. Able to raise legs against gravity, and head control and general muscle power better than case in Fig. 4.17 *(a, b)*. Clinical appearance somewhat similar to that of spinal muscular atrophy *(c)*. Needle biopsy of quadriceps showed marked vacuolar change in fibres *(d)*, with intense PAS stain for glycogen *(e)*. Diagnosis confirmed with biochemical analysis of muscle showing gross excess of glycogen and absent acid maltase.

Over the past few years a number of mild cases of type II glycogenosis with an identical deficiency of acid maltase in the muscle have been documented; there is only a mild proximal myopathy, resembling a limb girdle dystrophy, and usually no evidence of severe cardiac involvement, so there is correspondingly good prognosis. Histologically the muscle shows a vacuolar myopathy similar to that in the severe form.

Diagnosis. In the severe form the diagnosis may be suspected if cardiomegaly and hepatomegaly are found in association with a clinical picture resembling severe spinal muscular atrophy (Werdnig-Hoffmann disease), in which cardiomegaly is not a feature. The *electrocardiogram* shows a characteristic abnormality, with gigantic QRS complexes and a very short P-R interval. *Electromyography* may show a predominantly myopathic or a predominantly denervation pattern, but may also demonstrate a feature characteristic of type II glycogenosis, namely pseudomyotonic bursts, resembling the spontaneous myotonic bursts seen in myotonic syndromes, but not showing the characteristic waning of the action potentials. The excess glycogen is readily apparent on *muscle biopsy*, even in mild cases. Light microscopy shows a marked vacuolar myopathy, with complete distortion of the muscle pattern, and PAS-positive glycogen can be demonstrated in the vacuoles (Fig. 4.17). On electron-microscopy the sequestration of glycogen in membrane-bound spaces (Fig. 4.17) in type II glycogenosis has been observed by a number of authors, and supports the prediction of Hers (1963) that the glycogen would be lysosomal in distribution because acid maltase is a lysosomal enzyme.

Therapeutic possibilities. The possibility of replacement of deficient lysosomal enzyme in lipid envelopes (liposomes), which can be given intravenously and presumably will be taken up by the lysosomes of the liver, has been tried in the case described in Figure 4.17 (Tyrrell *et al.* 1976). Although there was a reduction in the liver size clinically, and there may have been some possible reduction in liver glycogen storage, the therapy did not influence the fatal outcome for the child, who was already in a terminal stage of cardiac failure. It may be worth trying at an earlier stage of the disease. An attempt was also made to treat the second child referred to above (Fig. 4.18) but unfortunately she developed acute pneumonia and died before the liposomes were ready.

Type III glycogenosis

Type III glycogenosis also affects both liver and skeletal muscle, but is much more benign than the classical type II (Fig. 4.19). Because of the absence of the debrancher enzyme, the glycogen has an abnormal structure with very short side chains (limit dextrin).

Skeletal muscle is usually only mildly affected in type III glycogenosis, and affected children may present with hypotonia and weakness. However, the effects of the hepatic involvement are likely to be more serious from the child's point of view, and clinical presentation is often with hypoglycaemia and ketosis. Hepatomegaly and delayed development may be present in early infancy, but the hepatomegaly can resolve spontaneously by adolescence, with eventual normal development, despite the persistence of the underlying enzymic defect.

67

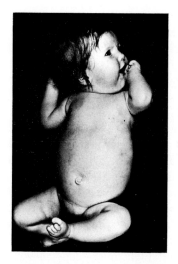

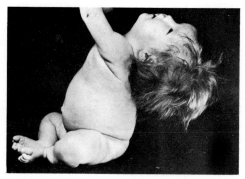

Fig. 4.19a *(left)*, **4.18b** *(above)*

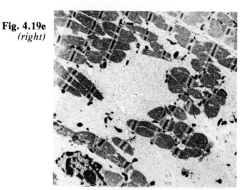

Fig. 4.19e
(right)

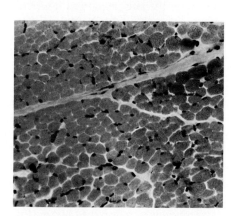

Fig. 4.19f
(right).

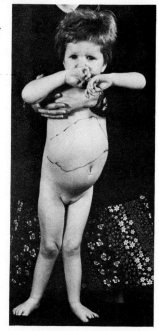

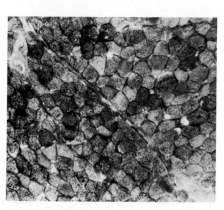

Fig. 4.19c *(above left)*, **4.19d** *(below left)*. *For caption see facing page.*

Diagnosis. Serum enzymes and EMG are usually normal and the muscle biopsy may also show a normal histological appearance, but excess glycogen may be suspected on PAS staining and confirmed by electronmicroscopy (Fig. 4.19). The definitive diagnosis is confirmed by demonstrating the enzyme deficiency in muscle or liver biopsy or in the leucocytes.

Management. Frequent small feeds and a high protein intake may help to prevent hypoglycaemia (Fernandes and van de Kamer 1968).

Course and prognosis. The condition seems to run a fairly mild course in many cases and there may even be a tendency towards improvement with time (see Fig. 4.19).

Type IV glycogenosis

This is a rare form of glycogenosis and the evidence for skeletal muscle involvement in various case reports has been conflicting. Thus the case of Holleman *et al.* (1966), who was ill from birth, had muscle weakness in addition to gross liver and splenic enlargement and died at the age of 6½ months. Autopsy examination showed mixtures of various amylopectin-like polysaccharides in liver, spleen and heart, and also in striated muscle. In contrast, in the two-year-old child with type IV glycogenosis reported by Brown and Brown (1966, 1968) the glycogen in the skeletal muscle was found to be normal, both in amount and in structure. The liver contained glycogen of abnormal structure and showed a deficit of branching enzyme. The 25-month-old child described by Reed *et al.* (1968) also showed no abnormal glycogen deposition in skeletal muscle. A sibling of the case of Holleman *et al.* (1966) was subsequently reported by Fernandes and Huijing (1968). This five-month-old child made few spontaneous movements, had poor muscle tone and the tendon reflexes were depressed. They were able to demonstrate a deficiency of branching enzyme in the leucocytes, but did not study the muscle. The case of Schochet *et al.* (1970) had generalized muscle wasting and associated muscle weakness, and there was biopsy as well as autopsy evidence of deposits of polysaccharide in the muscle. Biochemical assay of the muscle at biopsy, however, gave a normal value for glycogen content.

Abnormalities of lipid metabolism

Since muscle uses lipid as an alternative to carbohydrate as a source of energy, one might anticipate finding disorders of muscle associated with a defect in lipid metabolism, and this has been borne out in recent years.

Carnitine deficiency

Carnitine (γ-trimethyl amino-β-hydroxybutyrate) is present in high concentration

Fig. 4.19. Type III glycogenosis (limit dextrinosis). Four-month-old infant with hypotonia from birth and good movements of limbs but poor head control *(a, b)*. Gross hepatomegaly and mild cardiomegaly suggested glycogenosis and associated hypoglycaemia type III. Quadriceps biopsy showed reasonably normal-looking muscle *(c)*, with slight excess glycogen stain on PAS *(d)*. Excessive glycogen storage and loss of myofibrils striking in EM picture *(e)* and diagnosis confirmed biochemically by gross excess glycogen and absence of amylo-1,6-glucosidase (debrancher enzyme). Subsequently she showed steady improvement in motor ability and at four years was able to stand with support, although still hypotonic *(f)*. There was still marked hepatomegaly, but she remained free of hypoglycaemia on frequent, small, carbohydrate meals.

in muscle and acts as a carrier for long-chain fatty acids from the cytoplasm into the mitochondria, where they undergo β-oxidation.

Engel and Angelini (1973) first demonstrated carnitine deficiency in the muscle of a 23-year-old woman who had had weakness all her life, which had progressed from the age of 19. Muscle biopsy showed a vacuolar myopathy filled with lipid droplets on histochemical staining.

Additional cases have since been documented, usually presenting with muscle weakness but occasionally with associated neurological or hepatic manifestations.

The 11-year-old boy reported by Karpati et al. (1975) had always been clumsy and weak and had had floppiness of the head and neck since infancy. He had recurrent episodes of hepatic and cerebral dysfunction (encephalopathy). Carnitine deficiency was demonstrated in the muscle, serum and liver. The muscle biopsy showed lipid storage but the liver did not. Treatment of this child with DL-carnitine by mouth produced clinical improvement and an elevated level of plasma carnitine, but not of liver or muscle carnitine levels. Karpati and colleagues looked upon this as a syndrome of systemic carnitine deficiency, but thought that the recurrent and reversible cerebral manifestations, as well as the initial hypoglycaemia, might be secondary to the hepatic failure. It is possible, however, that the carnitine deficiency might have a direct effect on the nervous system.

Since carnitine is synthesized in the liver and secondarily distributed to other tissues, it is possible that a defect in hepatic carnitine synthesis could result in the reduced levels in muscle, plasma and liver.

Smyth et al. (1975) documented an 11-year-old boy with onset of weakness at 5½ years and associated neurological abnormalities. VanDyke et al. (1975) reported an eight-year-old boy with slowly progressive proximal weakness from the age of 18 months, but with no neurological abnormality. ECG showed evidence of associated cardiac involvement, which had not been documented in any previous case reports. Muscle carnitine was low but the serum carnitine normal, suggesting a possible abnormality in the entry of carnitine into the muscle. Treatment of the child with alternate-day prednisone (about 80mg) resulted in a definite improvement in muscle strength, but there was no change in the muscle biopsy performed five months later. The prednisone dosage was gradually reduced to 10mg without loss of the improved muscle strength. The family history was negative, but biopsies from the clinically normal parents showed a reduction of muscle carnitine to 23 per cent of normal (mean) in the mother and 34 per cent of normal in the father, compared with 10 per cent of normal in the affected child. This suggests an autosomal recessive mode of inheritance, both parents being heterozygotes. Partial carnitine deficiency in the muscle is also a feature of the mitochondrial-lipid-glycogen myopathy (see above)

Carnitine palmityl transferase deficiency
Carnitine palmityl transferase is an enzyme which catalyzes the reversible reaction of carnitine and long-chain fatty acyl groups. Carnitine palmityl transferase deficiency usually presents in later life with cramps and myoglobinuria and is unlikely to be involved in the floppy infant syndrome.

Periodic paralysis

This group of disorders is characterized by attacks of paralysis associated with flaccidity and there is a tendency to remission and relapse. Different types are recognized, depending on whether the serum potassium is low, high or normal during the attack.

Hypokalaemic periodic paralysis usually occurs during the second decade and has a peak incidence in early adult life, whereas the hyperkalaemic form is more likely to occur in infancy and childhood (Gamstorp 1956). In the hyperkalaemic type there may be associated myotonia. The predominant feature in both types is the attacks of weakness, which may occur during a period of rest after severe exercise or be provoked during exposure to cold, or by a heavy meal in the hypokalaemic form or by missing a meal in the hyperkalaemic form.

Diagnosis is confirmed by demonstrating the abnormal potassium levels. However, attacks can occur in the hyperkalaemic form with levels under 5mmol/l and severe paralysis may develop with levels of only 7mmol/l, which would not cause symptoms in normal subjects. This suggests that the potassium level is a secondary phenomenon and that the underlying metabolic abnormality remains to be resolved.

The frequency of attacks may vary considerably; some patients only have occasional attacks, whereas others have frequent daily attacks and are hardly ever free of some residual weakness.

In spite of the severity of the weakness, respiratory involvement is not a usual feature of attacks and death during an attack has not been recorded. However, Carson and Pearson (1964) reported a case of hyperkalaemic paralysis who had severe respiratory difficulty and lost consciousness. Treatment of the hyperkalaemic attacks has ranged from intravenous calcium gluconate and glucose infusion to various diuretics such as acetazolamide or hydrochlorothiazide (particularly for prevention of attacks), and recently salbutamol by inhalation has been used as a means of prophylaxis.

CHAPTER 5

Other Neuromuscular Disorders

Congenital myotonic dystrophy

The classical syndrome of myotonic dystrophy is essentially an adult disorder, but may have its onset in childhood. However, in recent years the congenital form of myotonic dystrophy has been recognized with increasing frequency as a fairly common and important contributor to the floppy infant syndrome. Vanier (1960) first drew attention to it, and subsequent reports have highlighted the fairly consistent clinical features. Harper and Dyken (1972) and Dyken and Harper (1973) reviewed a series of cases in the United States, and subsequently Harper (1975a, b) undertook a detailed study of all available cases in Great Britain, comprising some 70 patients from 54 sibships.

Clinical features

The main presenting features in the newborn period are general hypotonia and difficulty with sucking and swallowing, usually to a degree requiring tube feeding. Some cases may also have severe respiratory difficulties (which can be fatal) or associated deformities such as talipes equinovarus. A history of hydramnios during pregnancy is also a common feature and is presumably due to the inability of the fetus to swallow amniotic fluid *in utero* (Dunn and Dierker 1973, Moosa 1974). The mother may also have noted diminished fetal movements.

On clinical examination these infants have a striking facial diplegia, usually associated with an open, triangular mouth and inability to close the eyes fully (Figs. 5.1-5.3). Myotonia is not a feature of the condition at this stage and is also not usually detectable on EMG. Skeletal deformities are common, particularly talipes and kyphoscoliosis (Figs. 5.1-5.3).

The diagnosis is confirmed by examination of the mother, who will almost invariably show subclinical or overt features of dystrophia myotonica, although she is usually symptom-free. The two most consistent signs are mild facial weakness, with inability to screw the eyes closed and bury the eyelashes (Figs. 5.1-5.3), and clinical myotonia after clenching the fist. The myotonia can be confirmed in the mother on EMG, particularly in more distal muscles such as the interossei.

There is a high incidence of death from *respiratory failure* in these cases, many of which may go undiagnosed. Harper (1975a) observed an unusually high rate of neonatal mortality in siblings of his cases; many of these had been associated with hydramnios as well as talipes, and in retrospect were presumptive cases of dystrophia myotonica. There have also been autopsy reports of *hypoplasia of the diaphragm* (Aicardi *et al.* 1974, Bossen *et al.* 1974), which may be suspected on an X-ray showing diaphragmatic elevation. The presence of thin ribs on chest X-ray was noted by Bell and Smith (1972) and led to the retrospective diagnosis in two siblings who died of

72

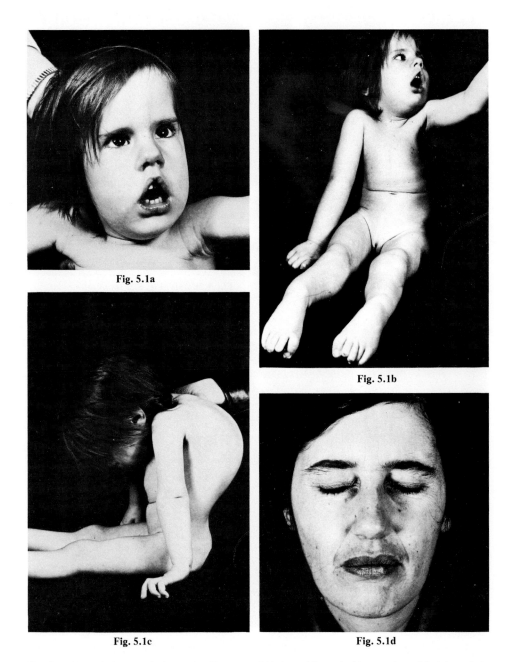

Fig. 5.1a

Fig. 5.1b

Fig. 5.1c

Fig. 5.1d

Fig. 5.1. Congenital myotonic dystrophy. Two-year-old infant with marked hypotonia and facial paralysis, with tent-shaped mouth *(a)* from birth, fixed talipes of feet *(b)* and marked kyphosis *(c)*. Transitory sucking and swallowing difficulty in first few weeks. Subsequent gradual improvement of hypotonia; able to sit unaided by two years and to walk at 4½ years. Her mother had mild facial weakness and inability to bury the eyelashes on screwing up her eyes *(d)*; EMG showed marked myotonia.

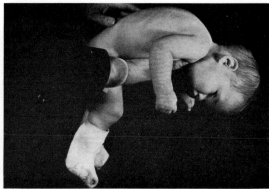

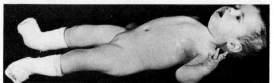

Fig. 5.2a   **Fig. 5.2b** *(top)*, **Fig. 5.2c** *(bottom)*

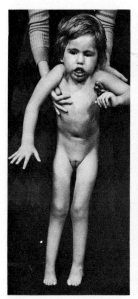

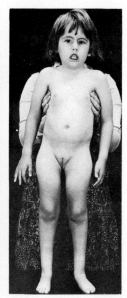

Left to right:
Figs. 5.2d, 5.2e, 5.2f

Fig. 5.2. Congenital myotonic dystrophy. Seven-month-old infant with marked hypotonia and transitory feeding difficulty in neonatal period, showing tent-shaped mouth *(a)*. Fixed talipes equinovarus affected both feet and she had a moderate kyphosis *(b. c)*. Her hypotonia and motor function gradually improved and she was able to support her weight after the age of three years *(d. e)* and to walk with support by five years *(f)*. She required operative procedures to straighten the feet. Facial appearance persisted *(g)*. Her mother was symptom-free but had myopathic-looking facies, was unable to screw up her eyes tightly and bury her eyelashes, and showed mild myotonia on closure of hands, with striking myotonic bursts on EMG.

74

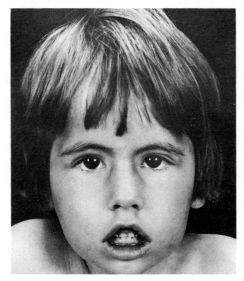

Fig. 5.2g

respiratory distress in the newborn period: their mother and one surviving sibling were then found to have dystrophia myotonica (Fried *et al.* 1975).

There is usually no clinical evidence of *cardiomyopathy*, but the ECG may show abnormality in some of these cases. A recent review of five of our own cases aged between seven months and six years showed an abnormal ECG, suggestive of right ventricular hypertrophy, in two (aged two and three years).

Lenard *et al.* (1977) demonstrated an associated involvement of *smooth muscle*, manifesting as megacolon and associated bowel symptoms, in two brothers with congenital myotonic dystrophy.

Mental retardation is a common feature of the congenital form of dystrophia myotonica. Some cases do fall within the normal range but in general there is a marked shift to the left in the range of mental ability, as in the case of Duchenne dystrophy but more exaggerated. The mental retardation is not progressive.

Clinical course

Infants with congenital dystrophia myotonica show a gradual improvement in hypotonia and will eventually walk, although this may be considerably delayed (Fig. 5.2). The facial diplegia persists, and they subsequently develop clinical and EMG evidence of myotonia and later show progressive features of the adult form of the disease. Those with respiratory distress usually tend to improve once they get past the neonatal period. The sucking and swallowing difficulties usually resolve in about eight to 12 weeks.

Harper (1975*b*, 1979) has suggested that the most likely explanation for the congenital form of dystrophia myotonica, with its transitory hypotonia and neonatal problems, is an additional maternal intra-uterine factor affecting those individuals who already have the dominant gene for myotonic dystrophy.

75

Diagnosis

Special investigations are unlikely to be helpful in confirming the diagnosis of myotonic dystrophy in the affected infant. EMG is usually negative and muscle biopsy usually shows only mild changes, predominantly atrophy of muscle fibres, particularly the type 1 fibres, and possibly some minor changes on electronmicroscopy. In later childhood, however, muscle biopsy may show more striking pathological features, resembling some of the changes classically found in the adult type of myotonic dystrophy.

On the other hand, the diagnosis is usually easy to confirm in the mother, particularly with electromyography. EMG and clinical evidence of myotonia also become apparent in the affected child in later childhood.

Management

The main risk of death is within the early newborn period as a result of respiratory failure and the complications of swallowing difficulties. If the child survives the newborn period the prognosis for survival is good.

It is important to treat such skeletal deformities as talipes and scoliosis and to try to prevent their progression, as they may be an important factor in the general mobility of the child later.

As myotonia is not an important feature in these infants, there is no indication for specific drug therapy for this symptom.

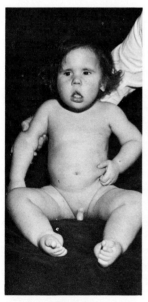
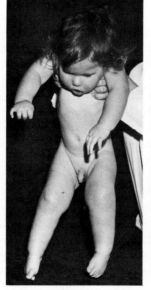
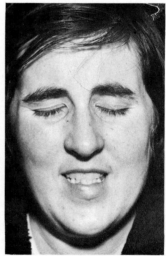

| Fig. 5.3a | Fig. 5.3b | Fig. 5.3c |

Fig. 5.3. Congenital myotonic dystrophy. 18-month-old infant with gradually resolving severe hypotonia from birth, able to sit unsupported *(a)* but unable to stand *(b)*. (Note tent-shaped triangular mouth.) His symptom-free mother had a somewhat expressionless face, was unable to bury her eyelashes *(c)* and EMG readily elicited myotonia in her but not in the child.

Genetic counselling

The condition is inherited through an autosomal dominant mechanism and there is thus a 50 per cent risk of further infants being affected. Presumably the transitory hypotonia and associated features are due to an additional factor superimposed on the basic disease pattern, and all these infants will manifest features of the adult type of disease as they grow older.

Careful examination of other members of the family will often reveal subclinical cases.

In view of the high incidence of neonatal deaths among siblings of index cases of congenital myotonic dystrophy (Harper 1975*a*), it would appear that if one infant is affected with the congenital form of myotonic dystrophy then a subsequent affected infant is likely to manifest the same severity of disorder rather than present at a later age with the adult type of myotonic dystrophy.

Antenatal diagnosis

The gene for dystrophia myotonica has been shown to be on the same chromosome as the secretor gene for ABO blood-group substances (Mohr 1954, Renwick *et al.* 1971, Harper *et al.* 1972). This means that in a small proportion of affected families who have the appropriate secretor status and associated myotonic dystrophy, it may be possible on the basis of the secretor status of the fetus to predict from amniocentesis whether that fetus is likely to be affected by myotonic dystrophy.

Antenatal treatment

If the hypotonic syndrome developing *in utero* is due to a circulating antibody which crosses the placenta (analogous to the situation in myasthenia gravis), theoretically it would seem feasible to treat a pregnant woman with plasmapharesis in order to reduce the circulating antibody and presumably protect the infant. Although no such antibody has been identified, it may be justified to try this form of therapy if a previous infant has been severely affected and genetic linkage studies have suggested that the subsequent fetus is also going to be affected by myotonic dystrophy.

Congenital muscular dystrophy

This term has been widely used for a group of infants with weakness, usually associated with hypotonia from birth, and a muscle biopsy showing striking pathological changes similar to a muscular dystrophy. Contractures of various muscles are often present and the infant may present with a clinical picture of 'arthrogryposis'.

Despite the name and the striking pathological picture, the condition usually tends to remain relatively static or progresses only very slightly, and indeed some cases may actually improve with time, pass various motor milestones and achieve the ability to walk. The name is thus a misnomer, but it is difficult to suggest an alternative since a non-specific term such as 'congenital myopathy' is unhelpful and overlaps with other non-specific myopathies lacking the same striking dystrophic picture. In addition, it seems as though congenital muscular dystrophy is a distinct genetic entity, with an autosomal recessive pattern of inheritance.

Although one might have had the impression from the literature up to relatively

Fig. 5.4a

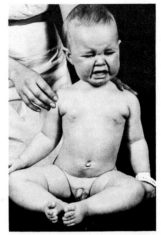

Fig. 5.4b

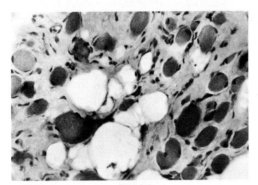

Fig. 5.4c

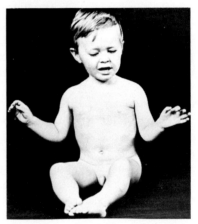

Fig. 5.4d

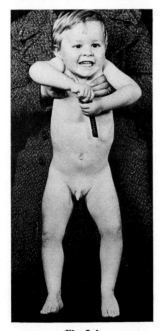

Fig. 5.4e

Fig. 5.4. Congenital muscular dystrophy. Nine-month-old infant with marked hypotonia and weakness from birth, still with poor head control *(a)* and ability to sit with support *(b)*. He was unable to stand with support and legs were still very floppy. He had no contractures. CPK was 1200 iu/l and EMG was myopathic. Muscle biopsy of quadriceps showed a strikingly dystrophic picture, with marked loss of muscle fibres and replacement by fat and connective tissue *(c)*. He showed steady improvement and by two years was sitting without support *(d)* and able to stand with support *(e)*. Subsequently able to walk unaided by 4 years and developed flexion contractures at the hips *(f, g)*.

recent times, mainly of single case reports, that the disorder was extremely rare, that is not the case: such an impression probably reflects the lack of adequate investigation in previous cases presenting with hypotonia in the newborn period, or with arthrogryposis.

In recent years there have been several reviews of larger series of cases which have defined more clearly a clinical pattern of disease, and also highlighted some striking differences.

Vassella *et al.* (1967) described eight cases in detail and reviewed 27 from the literature. They defined congenital muscular dystrophy as a primary myopathy already present at birth, with the same features as seen in progressive muscular dystrophy. They drew attention to the variability in clinical severity and also to the high incidence of affected siblings, suggesting an autosomal recessive pattern of inheritance. Zellweger and colleagues reported three cases of benign congenital muscular dystrophy and, in a separate paper, three with a severe form of disease (Zellweger *et al.* 1967*a, b*). The exact criteria for the subdivision into benign and severe are not clear, since one of the severe cases did achieve the ability to walk. Rotthauwe *et al.* (1969) reviewed eight personal cases, using the same diagnostic criteria as Vassella and colleagues. They categorized seven as severe and one as benign. All had weakness and hypotonia at birth, and sucking and swallowing difficulty was also common. It is difficult to get a clear picture of the clinical course in individual cases, as this is not summarized or tabulated, but it would appear that several of them achieved the ability to walk. The oldest cases were a brother and sister aged 14 and 23 years. Their case 8 showed improvement from the age of 18 months

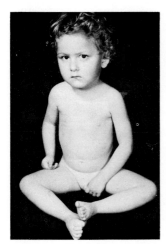

Fig. 5.5a

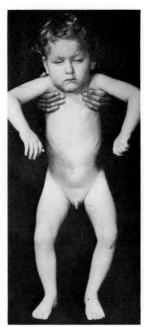

Figs. 5.5b *(right)*, 5.5c *(far right)*

Fig. 5.5. Congenital muscular dystrophy. 3½-year-old boy with hypotonia from birth and numerous contractures. Able to sit unsupported *(a)* and to take some weight on legs *(b, c)*. Improvement in range of joint movements after treatment with passive movement and intensive physiotherapy, and achieved ambulation with lightweight calipers. Muscle biopsy showed advanced dystrophic change.

and was able to walk unaided by 2½ years. The biopsy section shows two populations of fibres, and in the absence of histochemical studies one cannot be sure that this was not a case of congenital fibre type disproportion rather than muscular dystrophy. Serum creatine phosphokinase (CPK) in this series was either normal or only slightly elevated.

Donner *et al.* (1975) reviewed 15 cases of congenital muscular dystrophy from Finland, followed for up to 15 years. These constituted 9 per cent of 160 cases of neuromuscular disorders seen at the same hospital over a 10-year period. Muscle weakness was generalized and included the face and respiratory muscles. Contractures were present at birth in nine and were amenable to treatment. There was a tendency for new contractures to develop in the second and third years. CPK tended to be high in the early stages (one to two years) and normal or near-normal later. Histopathological changes varied from slight to very extensive, or apparently inactive or burntout. Seven of their cases achieved the ability to walk unaided. Two died. ECG abnormalities were noted in three. The IQ range was from 78 to 130. The authors concluded that the active phase of the disease process was at its height during intrauterine or early postnatal life and then tended to wane, leaving a burnt-out state in which new contractures might develop and cause deterioration with time. Two families contained more than one affected child and in a third family the parents were first cousins, supporting an autosomal recessive inheritance.

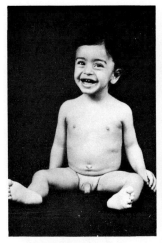

Fig. 5.6a

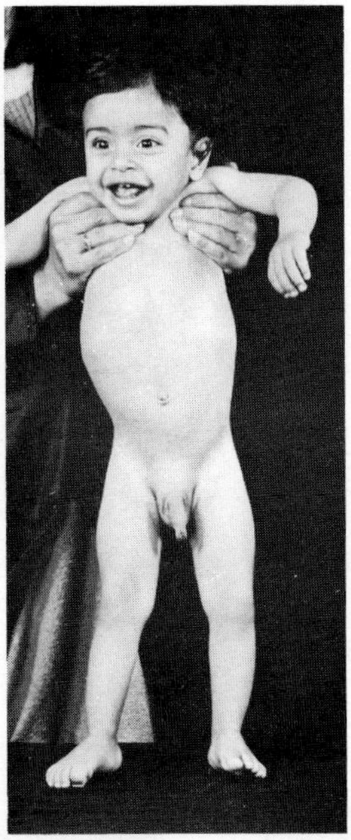

Fig. 5.6b

Fig. 5.6. Congenital muscular dystrophy. Two-year-old boy with marked hypotonia and weakness from birth, who steadily improved. Able to sit unaided *(a)* and to take weight on legs *(b)*, but still with poor head control *(c)*. Biopsy showed advanced changes of congenital dystrophy, with marked replacement of muscle by adipose tissue *(d)*.

Fig. 5.6c

Fig. 5.6d

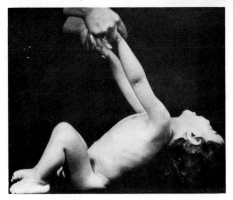

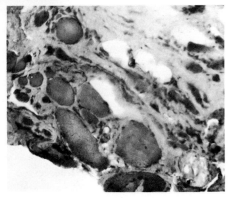

From my own unit, we have recently reviewed 27 of our cases, with particular reference to the management of some of the orthopaedic problems (Jones *et al.* 1979).

Several publications from Japan in recent years have reviewed over 100 cases of congenital muscular dystrophy, suggesting that the condition may be more prevalent there (Fukuyama *et al.* 1960, Matsumoto *et al.* 1970, Segawa 1970, Segawa *et al.* 1970, Nonaka *et al.* 1972). The type originally described in 15 cases by Fukuyama *et al.* (1960) is distinctive because of the associated severe mental retardation, and often febrile or afebrile convulsions. The muscular dystrophy itself affects the facial as well as the limb muscles and has the usual associated joint contractures.

Another form of congenital muscular dystrophy which may be a distinct entity

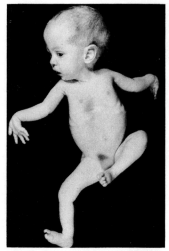

Fig. 5.7a

Fig. 5.7b

Fig. 5.7. Congenital muscular dystrophy/arthrogryposis. Six-month-old infant with very marked hypotonia from birth and with respiratory distress and feeding difficulty. Subsequently had recurrent life-threatening respiratory infections. Note marked deformities of hands, pectus excavatum and gross head lag *(a, b)*. CPK normal (51 iu/l), EMG myopathic. Muscle biopsy showed strikingly pathological picture with marked variability in fibre size and many whorled fibres *(c)*.

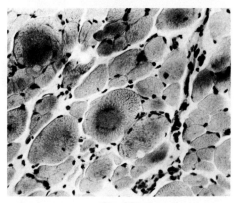

Fig. 5.7c

was reported by Lebenthal *et al.* (1970); there were 23 cases from a large Arab kindred and it was characterized by associated patent ductus arteriosus.

Santavuori *et al.* (1977) described a syndrome comprising congenital muscular dystrophy, mental retardation and ocular abnormality in nine children, including two brothers, and suggested it may be genetically determined through an autosomal recessive mechanism.

Clinical picture

From the published reports and from personal experience, one can probably draw the following picture of congenital muscular dystrophy (Figs. 5.4-5.8). The condition presents from birth with marked hypotonia and associated weakness affecting the limb, trunk and facial muscles. There may be associated sucking and swallowing difficulty and occasionally respiratory problems. In a large proportion of cases, contractures of various muscles are already present at birth ('arthrogryposis'); in others the contractures may develop later. The contractures tend to be progressive. Intellectual impairment and cardiac involvement are not integral features of the disease but are occasionally present. The weakness tends to be relatively static and

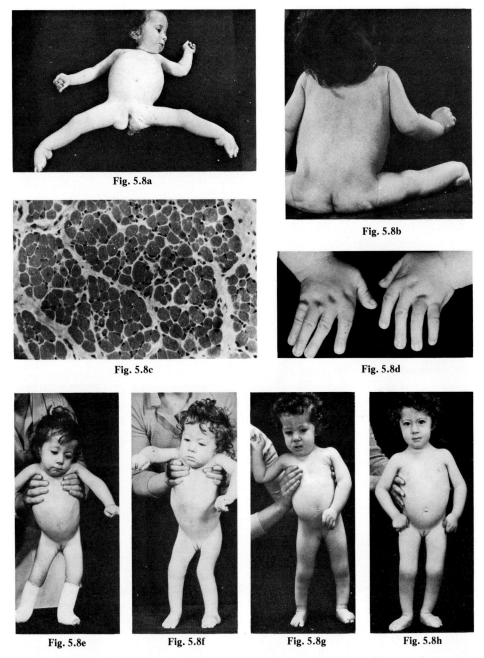

Fig. 5.8a

Fig. 5.8b

Fig. 5.8c

Fig. 5.8d

Fig. 5.8e   **Fig. 5.8f**   **Fig. 5.8g**   **Fig. 5.8h**

Fig. 5.8. Congenital muscular dystrophy/arthrogryposis. Six-month-old infant with severe limb contractures and deformities from birth. (Breech presentation with extended legs.) Muscle power good *(a)* and able to sit unaided *(b)*. Muscle biopsy showed mild myopathic change *(c)*. Marked improvement of flexion deformity of fingers following regular daily passive extension by parents *(d)*. Some improvement in flexed equinus deformity of feet but still needed operative correction *(e,* nine months). Gradual improvement in posture and function of legs *(f,* 12 months; *g.* 18 months; *h,* two years).

83

some cases actually may show improvement with time and pass motor milestones, although at a very delayed time. Walking may not be acquired until after the age of two years.

Investigations

Electromyography reveals a myopathic pattern. CPK may be moderately elevated, especially in the early phase, but can be within normal limits or only slightly elevated in the later phases. It usually does not attain the levels seen in Duchenne dystrophy.

Muscle biopsy always shows striking pathological changes, consistent with a dystrophic process. A striking feature of many biopsies is the remarkable replacement

Fig. 5.9. Minimal change myopathy/congenital muscular dystrophy. 20-month-old infant with hypotonia from birth. Able to sit unaided but not to stand *(a, b)*. EMG borderline abnormal, with occasional polyphasic potentials. Muscle biopsy showed minimal change; there was variation in fibre size but no abnormality. There was gradual improvement; he was able to stand unaided at six years but not to walk *(c, d)*. Persistent fixed flexion contractures at hips and knees *(d)*. Achieved ability to walk with calipers. Second biopsy obtained at time of tendo achilles tenotomy showed typical dystrophic picture, with marked variation in fibre size and replacement of muscle by fat or connective tissue *(e)*.

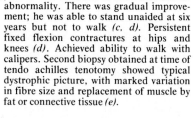

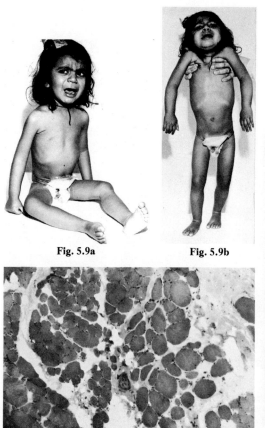

Fig. 5.9a   Fig. 5.9b

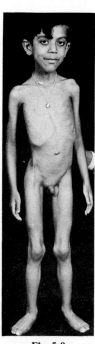 

Fig. 5.9e   Fig. 5.9c   Fig. 5.9d

of muscle by adipose tissue, and connective tissue proliferation is also usual. Some, however, show mainly connective tissue proliferation and little adipose tissue. The muscle biopsy often looks a lot worse than the clinical picture and one may be surprised that a patient with such extensive pathological change in a limb muscle may actually be ambulant. In no circumstances, therefore, should the biopsy picture be used as an index of severity of the disease or as a means of prognosis.

In some cases the pathological picture is much milder and may comprise mainly variation in fibre size, with little degenerative change or proliferation of fat and connective tissue. Supportive evidence that this is the same condition has come recently from a study of two siblings; the older child had a classical dystrophic picture in the muscle, whereas his younger sister, with much milder weakness, had minimal myopathic change. Similarly, in the case of a child with hypotonia and contractures from birth whom I had previously looked upon as minimal change myopathy, a subsequent muscle biopsy at the time of tenotomy of the tendo calcaneus showed an overt dystrophic picture (Fig. 5.9).

Genetics

Although a large number of the case reports have been isolated, sufficient affected siblings have now been documented, as has a high incidence of consanguinous marriage among the parents, to suggest an autosomal recessive inheritance in at least a proportion of cases. It would also appear that the syndrome with associated mental retardation and degenerative changes in the central nervous system, which appears to be common in Japan, is probably distinct from the syndrome unassociated with central nervous system involvement. Although rare in this country, occasional cases do show the classical Fukuyama syndrome with associated intellectual retardation.

Management

In view of the relatively static or non-progressive course the disease is likely to follow, it is important to try to correct existing contractures by passive stretching, night splints and serial plaster casts and to prevent progression of contractures by active and passive exercises. Some cases may need tenotomies in order to achieve an upright posture and consequent ambulation. It is better to do this early, once it becomes obvious that more conservative measures are unlikely to be adequate; otherwise the contractures may progress to a point where operative straightening of the limbs, particularly at the knees or hips, becomes impossible and may compromise the nerves and blood vessels.

The patient should be encouraged from an early stage to be mobile and active, since immobility is always conducive to progression of contractures. In late cases which have had no active treatment, one frequently finds that the fixed deformities of the limbs are more of a handicap than the degree of muscle weakness.

Some patients whose power is too weak to sustain their bodyweight may achieve ambulation with calipers, and the same principles apply as in the management of cases of spinal muscular atrophy of intermediate severity.

In cases of arthrogryposis with severe contractures from birth, my philosophy is to promote active mobility rather than to encourage persistence of the contractures by immobilizing these patients in plaster. The parents can be shown how to make active attempts to stretch the shortened tendons and it is surprising how much resolution one can get, even of apparently fixed deformities such as talipes equinovarus. Particular attention should also be paid to the hands, in which there is often limitation of extension of the wrists and fingers; the latter may be held in a tightly flexed position. With sustained, gentle pressure the fingers can often be fully extended, and if the parents persistently do this on a number of occasions every day the hands usually remain completely open and show a practically normal range of movement within a few weeks. Any surgical intervention should be delayed until it is certain that no more benefit can be achieved from passive movements. There is a tendency for recurrence of the deformity following surgery, so it is important initially to immobilise the joint in the corrected position, and once the plaster is removed to encourage passive movements through the full range of the joint to prevent this recurrence.

Duchenne muscular dystrophy

Although Duchenne muscular dystrophy does not usually show obvious clinical symptoms until after the child starts walking, hypotonia may be noted in early infancy (Fig. 5.10). There is often a lack of resistance of the muscle, and when lifted by the armpits the infant may 'slip through'. Careful observation may show evidence of minimal weakness in this 'pre-clinical' phase and there is frequently a delay in motor as well as intellectual milestones (Dubowitz 1965). Even if these features are not

Fig. 5.10a

Fig. 5.10. Duchenne muscular dystrophy. Two-year-old boy presenting with delayed motor milestones and hypotonia. Able to stand with support (a) but still showing poor head control (b). CPK 1310 iu/l, EMG myopathic and needle biopsy showed typical dystrophic changes.

Fig. 5.10b

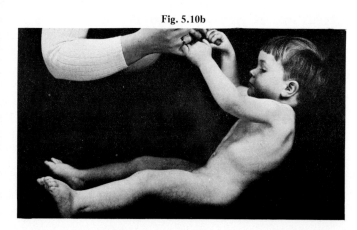

obvious to the physician, the mother with a previously affected child will often be convinced that a subsequent infant is already affected in the early months of life because he 'does not feel right' when handled.

Diagnosis can be readily confirmed by the greatly elevated levels of serum creatine phosphokinase and by the myopathic changes on electromyography and muscle biopsy.

Myasthenia

Neonatal myasthenia

This is a transient disorder in a potentially normal infant of a myasthenic mother and is the result of transplacental passage of antibody to the acetylcholine receptor-site of the neuromuscular junction.

The vast majority of infants born to myasthenic mothers are completely normal and require no treatment (Holt and Hansen 1951). However, about one in seven will be affected (Osserman 1958) and some may have severe, life-threatening weakness needing urgent treatment. Signs are usually present at or soon after birth, but occasionally may be delayed, so it is worth keeping these infants under close observation for perhaps a week.

Affected infants are usually limp, with generalized hypotonia and a sluggish or absent Moro response. Commonly associated features include difficulty in sucking and swallowing, difficulty with breathing, and ptosis and facial weakness.

There seems to be no correlation between the occurrence and severity of the infant's symptoms and the severity or duration of the mother's myasthenia, but Papatestas *et al.* (1973) found a two-fold higher incidence of neonatal myasthenia in women who had not had thymectomy compared with those who had. It is rare for successive infants of the same mother to be affected. The most likely explanation for the infant's involvement is the passage from the mother of antibody to acetylcholine receptor. Babies born to myasthenic mothers with high titres receive the IgC and are likely to be affected, whereas those born to mothers with low titres tend to be normal. There is still controversy about the correlation of myasthenia in the infant with the antibody titre in the mother, since only about 14 per cent of these infants are clinically affected while about 80 per cent of mothers would be expected to show significant titres.

Treatment should be commenced immediately in severely affected infants. Some mildly affected cases may settle spontaneously without treatment. Neostigmine bromide ('Prostigmin') in a dose of 1 to 5mg orally, depending on severity and response, should be given with the feeds and adjusted according to the response. When it cannot be readily given orally it may be given by intramuscular injection as neostigmine methyl sulphate. The progress usually can be monitored clinically, but for those who like a bit of sophistication the sucking pressure during feeding can be monitored with a balloon attached to a feeding tube (Hutchison *et al.* 1975).

The condition has a tendency to spontaneous remission, usually within two to four weeks, and once therapy has been tapered and stopped there is no risk of relapse.

If a high level of circulating antibody can be identified during the latter part of pregnancy, the risk to the infant could theoretically be lessened by treating the mother with plasma exchange to remove the circulating antibody, but this procedure may be potentially hazardous for the fetus.

Congenital or infantile myasthenia

Congenital myasthenia presenting in the newborn period in infants of non-myasthenic mothers is very rare. Macrae (1954) recorded an infant with weakness at birth whose fetal movements had been strikingly diminished in the last six weeks of pregnancy. Levin (1949) described two siblings with congenital myasthenia, of whom the second case was anticipated because of poor fetal movements during pregnancy. Further individual cases have been documented by Teng and Osserman (1956) and Gath *et al.* (1970).

More commonly, the onset of symptoms is after the neonatal period but within the first one to two years of life. The use of a cut-off point of two years to separate the early onset (infantile) from the later onset (juvenile) cases is an arbitrary one, but may have some genetic significance (Bundey 1972).

Clinical features. The clinical picture of myasthenia in infancy and childhood has been well documented by Teng and Osserman (1956) and Millichap and Dodge (1960). These cases usually present with ptosis and ophthalmoplegia but may develop more generalized muscle weakness later. The course tends to be more benign but also more persistent than the adult form. The good prognosis in the familial infantile form has been documented by a number of authors (Levin 1949, Kott and Bornstein 1969, Namba *et al.* 1971*a*). The course tends to be non-fluctuating and compatible with long survival and little need for medication.

However, a number of recent reports on fatal cases of congenital myasthenia suggest that the prognosis is not always good. McLean and McKone (1973) documented congenital myasthenia in identical female twins, with onset of progressive respiratory distress at 8 and 11 days respectively. Grunting respirations and weak cry were followed by pallor, cyanosis, generalized weakness, and by apnoea and unconsciousness due to pharyngeal/laryngeal obstruction. There was associated general weakness and ptosis but there was a good response to neostigmine 0.125mg intramuscularly and subsequent maintenance on oral pyridostigmine. At the age of 21 months twin 2 died after an acute attack of breathing difficulty followed by respiratory arrest. An older male sibling who had had similar spells of respiratory difficulty in the newborn period, thought to be seizures, died at the age of six months.

Conomy *et al.* (1975) described an 18-month-old infant who had had several episodes of dysphagia and respiratory distress with associated cyanosis from the age of three months. These were usually precipitated by an infection. The diagnosis was confirmed by the remarkable response to intravenous edrophonium and he was maintained on anticholinesterase medication, for which there was an increasing requirement. He continued to have episodes of weakness necessitating temporary increase in medication, precipitated by recurrent otitis media. A previous sibling had had a very similar history of episodic swallowing and breathing difficulty and had died in respiratory failure at 15 months of age without a diagnosis of myasthenia being made.

Oberklaid and Hopkins (1976) described a similar infant with onset at six months of swallowing and respiratory difficulties, progressing to respiratory arrest from retained secretions. There was associated hypotonia, ptosis and an expressionless face. She responded markedly to intramuscular neostigmine (0.25mg) and was maintained on oral pyridostigmine. At 10 months of age she had an acute episode of weakness, followed by vomiting, and died shortly afterwards despite intramuscular neostigmine.

These reports suggest that a common presentation of infantile myasthenia gravis may be with acute episodes of bulbar weakness and associated accumulation of pharyngeal secretions, with laryngeal obstruction and respiratory distress. These episodes can be life-threatening unless recognized and treated with appropriate medication.

In the isolated case of congenital or infantile myasthenia the diagnosis can be readily missed. The syndrome should always be kept in mind for the infant with unexplained swallowing or respiratory difficulty, particularly in the presence of associated ptosis, ophthalmoplegia or hypotonia. The diagnosis can then be confirmed by demonstrating a response to intravenous edrophonium (1mg). The response is usually almost instant but may only persist for a few minutes. Ophthalmoplegia is unlikely to respond but the ptosis, facial weakness or general weakness or hypotonia should show a change. At times it is difficult to be sure about a borderline response. As an alternative, neostigmine methyl sulphate, 0.125mg intramuscularly, can be used. Improvement might appear within 10 minutes, reach a maximum in 30 minutes and last for three to four hours. Where the result is equivocal the test can be repeated, perhaps with an increased dosage, and followed by a therapeutic trial of oral neostigmine.

Genetics. The detailed genetic studies of infantile and juvenile myasthenia gravis by Bundey (1972) suggest an autosomal recessive pattern of inheritance, and this is supported by the twin studies of Namba *et al.* (1971*b*).

Botulism

This disease resembles myasthenia gravis, since the botulinum toxin also affects neuromuscular transmission. It may occur in early infancy with acute hypotonia, weakness, ptosis and dysphagia (Pickett *et al.* 1976). Although relatively common in the United States (Black and Arnon 1977), the condition is practically unknown (or perhaps missed) in England (Turner *et al.* 1978). There has been a suggestion that honey contaminated with Cl. botulinum may have been a factor in a high proportion of infants with type B botulism affection (Arnon *et al.* 1979).

Peripheral neuropathies: (A) Acquired

Acquired lesions of the lower motor neurone are rare in infancy but may present as a floppy infant with weakness and hypotonia of the limbs.

Poliomyelitis

Poliomyelitis has always been rare in the neonatal period and early infancy, but cases are well documented (Mouton *et al.* 1950, Baskin *et al.* 1950, Shelokov and

Weinstein 1951) (Fig. 5.11). In the two cases of Baskin *et al.,* the disease appears to have been acquired from the affected mothers. Diagnosis may at times be easy if the weakness is focal or asymmetrical, but from reports in the literature about half the early cases appear to have presented with generalized flaccidity or hypotonia. With the virtual eradication of poliomyelitis in many countries by immunization, neonatal poliomyelitis will become even more rare, but sporadic cases may still occur. Other viruses, such as Coxsackie, may produce a similar picture.

A relatively acute onset of symptoms, together with signs of ill health and abnormality in the cerebrospinal fluid, may help to establish or exclude the diagnosis.

Polyneuropathy

In 1957 Chambers and MacDermot described three children with 'amyotonia congenita' due to polyneuritis. The first, a boy of 7½ years, developed generalized hypotonia and immobility of the limbs, particularly the legs, after gastro-enteritis at two months. Improvement was very slow and he eventually walked at four years. He was left with a quite considerable motor deficit. The second, a boy of four years, had delay in attaining early motor milestones but there had been gradual improvement, particularly after the age of three years. There was associated ataxia and loss of joint position sense and of two-point discrimination in the feet. The third case, a girl of 5½ years, had delay in reaching motor milestones, apparent after the age of six months,

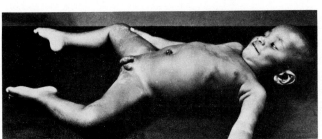

Fig. 5.11a

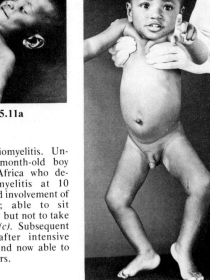

Fig. **5.11.** Poliomyelitis. Un-immunised 16-month-old boy from Central Africa who developed poliomyelitis at 10 months. Marked involvement of both legs *(a)*; able to sit unsupported *(b)* but not to take weight on legs *(c)*. Subsequent improvement after intensive physiotherapy and now able to walk with calipers.

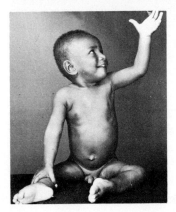

Fig. 5.11b

Fig. 5.11c

90

and did not walk until three years. She showed gradual improvement, but had residual weakness of the legs, ataxia and some associated sensory loss in the feet. In all three children, electromyography and muscle biopsy showed signs of denervation and protein in the cerebrospinal fluid was raised.

Byers and Taft (1957) described four children with chronic polyneuropathy, which tended to be progressive. In one child, weakness had been present since birth and there was delay in reaching all her motor milestones.

Infantile peripheral neuropathy may at times mimic Werdnig-Hoffmann disease; Goebel *et al.* (1976) reported such a case and also reviewed six similar cases from the literature. Kasman *et al.* (1976) documented a further three cases with onset in early infancy.

Infectious polyneuropathy (Guillain-Barré syndrome) may also occur in infancy (Debré and Thieffry 1951, Aylett 1954, Peterman *et al.* 1959) but is unlikely to present in the first year of life. It tends to have an acute onset, particularly with weakness of the legs, rather than generalized weakness or hypotonia. Cranial nerves may also be involved. Albumen in the cerebrospinal fluid is usually markedly elevated, without any increase in cells. Motor nerve conduction is slow.

Peripheral neuropathies: (B) Hereditary

This is a heterogeneous group of disorders based on classical descriptions of clinical syndromes, which still carry the eponymous titles of their authors, such as Charcot-Marie-Tooth disease for the peroneal muscular atrophy with dominant inheritance; the Roussy-Lévy variant of Charcot-Marie-Tooth disease; Dejerine-Sottas peripheral neuropathy with autosomal recessive inheritance; Refsum's disease with its associated retinopathy, ataxia, hearing loss, cardiomyopathy and other changes, and excess phytanic acid excretion; and various other combinations of peripheral neuropathy with other neurological signs. Dyck *et al.* (1975) tried to bring some order into the chaos by suggesting a systematic but somewhat cumbersome classification of these various syndromes into five types of hereditary motor and sensory neuropathy (HMSN) as follows:

HMSN type I — hypertrophic neuropathy (peroneal muscular atrophy);
HMSN type II — neuroneal type of peroneal muscular atrophy;
HMSN type III — hypertrophic neuropathy of infancy (Dejerine-Sottas);
HMSN type IV — hypertrophic neuropathy with excess phytanic acid (Refsum's disease);
HMSN type V — peripheral neuropathy with spastic paraplegia.

Hypertrophic neuropathy (peroneal muscular atrophy) (HMSN Type I)

The most common variety is HMSN type I, which is recognized by its very slow motor nerve conduction velocity and its dominant inheritance. This has been looked upon particularly as a disease of adult life, but with our routine investigation by nerve conduction velocity of both parents of every childhood case of peripheral neuropathy, we have been able to identify 15 childhood cases with proven dominant inheritance (Vanasse and Dubowitz 1980).

In addition, in some of these cases onset is in early infancy, or even already at

91

birth, and they usually present with mild weakness and some delay in attaining motor milestones. In general they are unlikely to present with the floppy infant syndrome.

Hypertrophic neuropathy of infancy (HMSN Type III)
    This is a recessively inherited disorder, usually with onset in infancy. There may be delay in passing early motor milestones and walking may only be achieved by the third or fourth year. After an initial improvement in motor function there is a gradual decline, and some patients may lose the ability to walk in adult life. Conduction velocity is markedly slowed in both the motor and the sensory nerves. It is important to check conduction velocity in both parents to exclude dominant inheritance.

Progressive degenerative disorders of the central nervous system
    The lower motor neurone is consistently involved in some of the progressive degenerations of the central nervous system. In the demyelinating leucodystrophies, such as metachromatic leucodystrophy and globoid cell leucodystrophy (Krabbe's disease), there is associated demyelination of the peripheral nerve, with resultant marked slowing of conduction velocity. The pattern of inheritance of these degenerative disorders is usually autosomal recessive.
    Metachromatic leucodystrophy (sulphatide lipidosis). The usual infantile form presents in the second year of life as a deterioration in motor and intellectual function in a previously normal child. The motor symptoms are often the presenting ones and there is a tendency to lose the ability to stand and walk, in association with hypotonia of the limbs and depression of the tendon reflexes (Fig. 5.12). Subsequently there is deterioration in intellectual function, progressive optic atrophy and blindness, and finally a state resembling decerebrate rigidity (Fig. 5.12).
    In the early stages there is already a marked slowing of motor nerve conduction velocity and the diagnosis can be confirmed by the demonstration of a marked reduction (or total absence) of the enzyme aryl sulphatase A in the leucocytes. A deposition of metachromatic material due to the accumulated sulphatide can be demonstrated in the sural nerve and also in nerves present in a muscle biopsy sample.
    The condition follows a steady downhill course and usually leads to death by about the age of five years.
    A more slowly progressive juvenile form also occurs, with a somewhat later onset and a more protracted course.
    Globoid cell leucodystrophy (Krabbe's disease). This form of leucodystrophy usually presents in the second half of the first year of life with a deterioration of motor and intellectual function, following a more acute course than the metachromatic leucodystrophy and often leading to death within a matter of months.
    Again the clinical diagnosis can be supported by the demonstration of markedly slowed nerve conduction velocity. In the past, confirmation of the diagnosis has usually been at autopsy, by demonstration of the characteristic globoid cells in the central nervous system. With the recent recognition of a specific enzyme deficiency (galactosyl-ceramide β-galactosidase), it may be possible in future to confirm the diagnosis more readily during life, and also to diagnose it antenatally.
    Neuraxonal dystrophy. This is also a progressive degenerative disorder of the

central nervous system, with onset in early infancy (Seitelberger 1952, Huttenlocher and Gilles 1967). A previously normal infant may present during the second year of life with muscle weakness and hypotonia, which may show a slowly progressive course. Usually there is also involvement of the corticospinal tracts. These children subsequently develop bulbar signs and visual impairment, and eventually die before reaching their teens.

Motor nerve conduction is not impaired (or may be slightly slowed). The characteristic histological abnormality on nerve biopsy is the presence of swellings along the course of the axon.

Other central nervous system disorders. Involvement of the lower motor neurone is a component of many of the other, somewhat rare, degenerative disorders of the nervous system. Marked slowing of motor nerve conduction and associated demyeli-

Fig. 5.12. Metachromatic leucodystrophy. Two-year-old girl presenting with hypotonia and difficulty with gait *(a, b)*. Able to sit unsupported but difficulty in standing and tendency to hyperextension of knees *(b)*. Milestones had previously been normal and intellect seemed unimpaired. Nerve conduction very slow (ulnar 14 m/sec, posterior tibial 10 m/sec). Clinical diagnosis of metachromatic leucodystrophy confirmed on intracellular metachromatic granules in freshly spun urinary deposit and absence of arylsulphatase A in leucocytes. She deteriorated steadily, developed decerebrate rigidity and marked intellectual impairment *(c, d)*, and died at 5½ years.

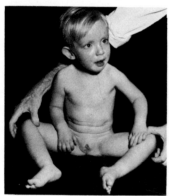

Fig. 5.12a

Fig. 5.12d

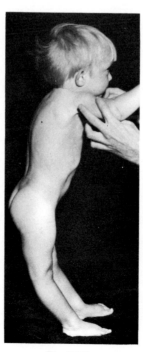

Fig. 5.12b

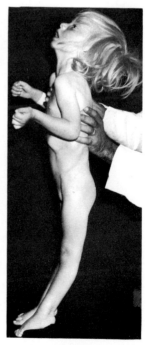

Fig. 5.12c

93

nation has been demonstrated in Cockayne's syndrome (Moosa and Dubowitz 1970) and in some cases of Leigh's syndrome (Moosa 1975). Hypotonia is a common component of the gangliosidoses, suggesting an associated involvement of the lower motor neurone, although there may be no overt abnormality in motor nerve conduction or electromyography. Recently Tomé and Fardeau (1976) demonstrated some abnormalities on electronmicroscopy. Hypotonia is also a common feature in familial dysautonomia and occurs as a non-specific manifestation of a wide variety of central nervous system disorders. In many of these conditions there is probably some functional disorder in the control of tone, rather than any direct involvement of the lower motor neurone itself.

PART II

NON-PARALYTIC DISORDERS

Hypotonia without Significant Weakness

There are many disorders outside the neuromuscular system which can produce hypotonia. These encompass a number of systems, and a wide range of diseases, and a complete differential diagnosis would cover practically all of paediatrics.

In many of these conditions the hypotonia is an incidental feature and the diagnosis will usually be suspected because of other clinical observations at the time of examination. In other conditions the hypotonia may be a prominent and presenting feature. I do not intend to draw up a complete list of all the conditions in which hypotonia may feature, but to concentrate on the disorders in which it is most likely to be a presenting symptom.

Little is yet known about how these diverse aetiological factors have a common effect on muscle tone. It is possible that they act through a common mechanism, perhaps with a relatively simple biochemical basis.

CHAPTER 6

Disorders of the Central Nervous System

In clinical practice this group forms a large segment of the children presenting with hypotonia as a primary symptom, or with delayed motor milestones and associated hypotonia. The majority of these cases, whatever the aetiology, also have mental retardation. This group can usually be recognized without difficulty on clinical grounds. In the first place, the child, although markedly hypotonic and floppy, will not be paralysed and will be able to move his limbs without difficulty. In addition to retardation in achieving motor milestones there will be evidence of delay in other developmental milestones, including those not dependent on motor ability. In some cases a specific clinical disorder may be obvious, such as Down's syndrome (trisomy 21) or a mucopolysaccharidosis, but in the majority the cause of the underlying mental deficiency is not apparent.

A careful assessment of the history is important. Any progression of mental retardation, particularly if milestones previously acquired have subsequently been lost, would suggest one of the progressive degenerative disorders of the central nervous system. The presence of associated clinical features may provide a clue to one of the syndromes associated with known abnormalities in metabolism, or to specific syndromes such as the Prader-Willi syndrome. A positive family history, particularly with a previously affected sibling, would also suggest an underlying metabolic disorder.

Non-specific mental deficiency

In the majority of children presenting with hypotonia, delay in motor milestones and mental retardation, no specific underlying cause can be found. In some there

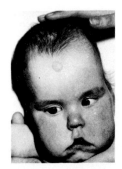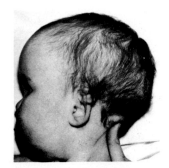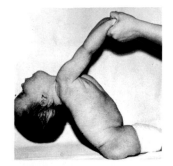

Fig. 6.1. 11-month-old infant with congenital hydrocephalus, mental retardation and marked hypotonia. Muscle biopsy completely normal.

may be marked microcephaly, while others may have a normal or even increased head circumference. Marked hypotonia can be an associated feature of hydrocephalus (Fig. 6.1) and also megalencephaly, sometimes with only relatively mild mental retardation.

The hypotonia varies considerably. In some cases there may be practically no recognizable tone in the muscle—an 'atonic' state—while in others hypotonia is minimal. The subsequent course is also variable. The child may remain grossly retarded and hypotonia may also persist, as in the case illustrated in Fig. 6.2. In others the tone improves in parallel with improvement in motor function.

There is an overlap between this group of cases and the group with so-called 'hypotonic cerebral palsy' with associated intellectual impairment. The diagnosis of cerebral palsy is usually based on the presence of associated features, such as athetosis, ataxia or exaggerated tendon reflexes.

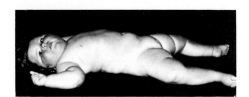

Fig. 6.2a

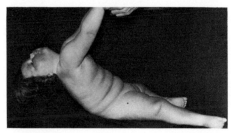

Fig. 6.2b

Fig. 6.2d

Fig. 6.2c

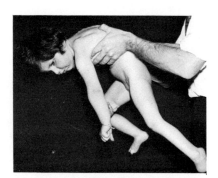

Fig. 6.2e

Fig. 6.2. Gross hypotonia and marked delay in motor milestones in 18-month-old infant with microcephaly and severe mental retardation. Note 'frog' posture in supine *(a)*, marked head lag on traction of hands *(b)* and poorly sustained posture in ventral suspension *(c)*. She remained hypotonic and grossly retarded and at five years *(d, e)* still had poor head control and posture and was unable to sit or to support her bodyweight on her legs. She also had athetoid movements and tendon reflexes were sluggish.

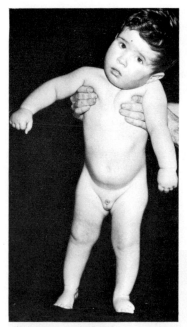

Fig. 6.3a

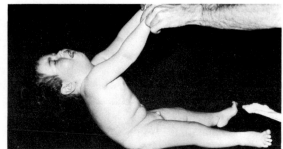

Fig. 6.3b

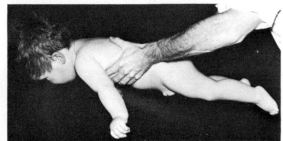

Fig. 6.3c

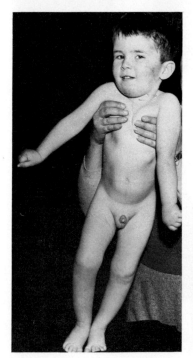

Fig. 6.3d

Fig. 6.3. Hypotonic 'cerebral palsy'. This child, born at term (forceps delivery) had delay in motor and intellectual milestones: when assesed at 19 months, muscle biopsy was histologically and histochemically normal. He had generallised hypotonia and was unable to support weight of his body *(a)*. There was marked head lag in supine *(b)* but better-maintained posture in ventral suspension *(c)*. No weakness or athetosis and tendon reflexes were absent. He showed some improvement in intellectual and motor development but by 2½ years was still unable to stand *(d)* and had poor head control *(e)*. He also developed marked ataxia and athetoid hand-movements.

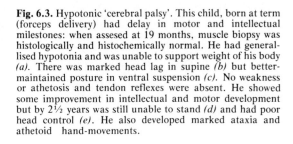

Fig. 6.3e

Hypotonic cerebral palsy

It is well documented that cerebral palsy, usually looked upon as a 'spastic' paralysis, may be associated with hypotonia rather than hypertonia, especially in the early phases.

Yannet and Horton (1952) reviewed 31 cases of hypotonic cerebral palsy associated with severe mental retardation in a training school for mentally retarded children. They subdivided them into three groups—atonic, ataxic and athetoid. In the atonic group, one child was found to have Tay-Sachs disease, two tuberous sclerosis and two had marked birth injury. In the ataxic group, one resulted from infantile encephalitis and two possibly had had kernicterus. In the athetoid group, five had siblings with a similar disorder. There was also a positive family history for three of the atonic and two of the ataxic children. All had exaggerated tendon jerks.

This must be a mixed group of disorders. Apart from the presence of athetosis, ataxia or exaggerated tendon jerks, there is no way of distinguishing the atonic group from cases with a non-specific mental retardation and associated hypotonia.

The combination of mental retardation and hypotonia, with or without brisk tendon jerks, athetosis or ataxia, is probably quite common. Therefore it is not surprising that cerebral palsy formed the largest diagnostic group in Richmond Paine's (1963) survey of 133 children, referred with delayed motor milestones and found to have incidental hypotonia.

In general I think the diagnosis of hypotonic cerebral palsy should be restricted to those hypotonic infants who also have exaggerated tendon reflexes or ankle clonus, or other features suggestive of 'cerebral palsy', such as athetosis (Fig. 6.3). Subdivision into ataxic or athetoid forms, if these features are striking, may be worthwhile since there may be a difference in pathogenesis and prognosis. In general, the severely retarded, grossly hypotonic cases (atonic type) do not show much improvement with time. A careful search should be made for underlying aetiological causes, particularly in familial cases. There is probably also overlap in presentation with some of the familial cerebellar ataxias, which may present in infancy as delay in passing motor milestones and with intellectual impairment, in addition to cerebellar signs (Jervis 1950).

Lesný (1979) recently documented a follow-up study of 98 cases of hypotonic cerebral palsy. The hypotonia tended to decrease with time and other syndromes emerged. The largest group developed cerebellar signs, followed by a group with 'developmental disintegration' and severe mental retardation. Spastic and/or dyskinetic signs developed in a small proportion, whereas another small group of patients showed marked improvement of the hypotonia but had residual minor signs of cerebral disturbance.

With more refined methods of screening for metabolic abnormalities in larger populations of retarded children, specific diagnoses will probably be established in future for many cases within this group. In addition, the wider application of such new, non-invasive techniques as ultrasonography and computerized tomography in the newborn period will help to identify intraventricular haemorrhage, cerebral atrophy and other pathological changes which may be associated with hypotonia in the newborn infant (Fig. 6.4).

Birth trauma, cerebral haemorrhage, hypoxia

Severe hypotonia is common in the newborn period following a difficult labour. It is a constant feature of the infant with severe asphyxia neonatorum. In these circumstances it is usually short-lived and disappears as the child's clinical condition improves.

Persistence of hypotonia may suggest intracranial haemorrhage, more lasting cerebral damage from hypoxia, or a focal lesion in the spinal cord. In the latter case there is likely to be associated paralysis.

In some infants extensor tone is disproportionately good compared with flexor tone. These infants will show gross head lag in the supine position, but good head posture in ventral suspension (Fig. 6.5). If it persists, this may be an early sign of cerebral palsy (Fig. 6.5). A similar disparity between extensor and flexor tone in the neck is observed following a face or brow presentation (Fig. 6.6), but this usually disappears within a few weeks. Infants delivered by the breech are particularly prone to injury of the cervical cord. In some of these cases of birth trauma, muscle weakness may be a prominent feature. The clinical picture may then resemble that of the paralytic group, as is well illustrated by the case in Fig. 6.7.

Perinatal drug influences

As a matter of general principle, one can assume that any drug given to the pregnant mother is likely to cross the placenta rapidly and enter the fetal circulation. This applies also to local anaesthetics given during labour (Dubowitz 1975). A number of drugs have been implicated in the production of hypotonia in the newborn infant; one commonly used such drug is diazepam. With our recently developed neonatal neurological assessment and documentation system (Dubowitz and Dubowitz 1980) we have been able to show a fairly consistent pattern in the newborn infant in relation to the administration of diazepam to the mother, even in relatively small doses. Hypotonia is a very striking and consistent feature and is out of proportion

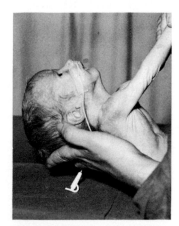

Fig. 6.4. Hypotonic preterm newborn infant with intraventricular haemorrhage identified by ultrasound skull examination.

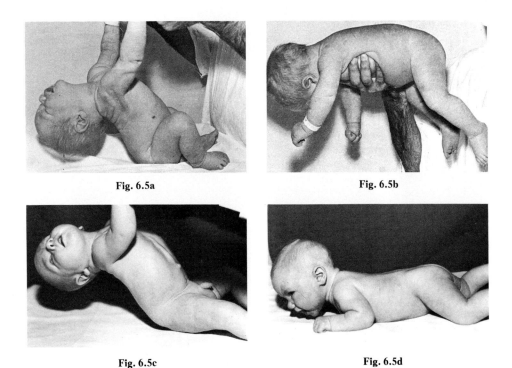

Fig. 6.5a

Fig. 6.5b

Fig. 6.5c

Fig. 6.5d

Fig. 6.5. Hypotonic newborn infant, born at term following difficult delivery. Thought to have intracranial haemorrhage. Note disproportionately severe head lag in supine *(a)* compared with ventral suspension *(b)*, suggesting relative increase in extensor tone. This disproportion persisted and at 10 weeks there was still marked head lag in supine *(c)* but relatively good head control in prone *(d)*.

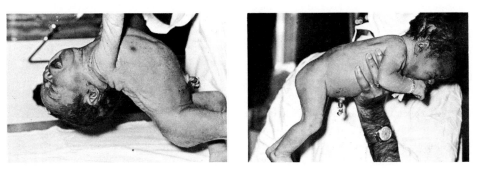

Fig. 6.6. Newborn full-term infant with face presentation, showing disproportionate tone in extensor muscles of neck compared with flexors. Tendency to hold head in hyperextended position persisted for about four weeks. The child also had transitory laryngeal stridor, presumably related to direct trauma to larynx during delivery.

101

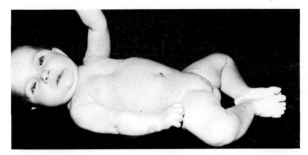

Fig. 6.7a

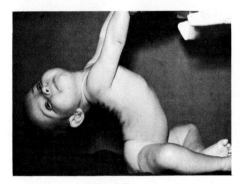

Fig. 6.7b

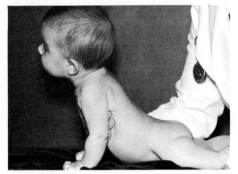

Fig. 6.7c

Fig. 6.7. Following breech delivery at term this child was blue, limp and apnoeic and needed intubation and positive pressure ventilation. Colour was maintained but chest movements were poor and breathing mainly diaphragmatic. There was minimal spontaneous limb movement and weak Moro response. On day six she developed urinary retention with overflow, which did not resolve until six weeks. Tone gradually improved after first week and spontaneous movements appeared, but after four months the legs seemed less mobile than before. When first seen at five months she had marked hypotonia, especially of legs, and 'frog' posture in supine *(a)*. She was barely able to sustain a leg momentarily against gravity. Breathing was mainly diaphragmatic and there was costal recession. She had marked head lag in supine *(b)* but good head control in prone *(c)*. Tendon reflexes were pathologically brisk; there was bilateral sustained ankle clonus and positive Babinski response. Diagnosis of cervical cord injury was confirmed on myelogram, which showed complete obstruction to flow from below at D1 and from above (cisternal puncture) at C8 vertebrae. An exploratory operation by the neurosurgeon showed marked stenosis of the dura at the level of C8 and T1 vertebrae and a very fibrous and atrophic segment of cord.

to any deviation in other neurological signs. Gillberg (1977) described a newborn infant with pronounced muscular hypotonia from birth as a result of persistently high levels of both diazepam and its metabolite desmethyldiazepam for the first 14 days of life. Initially there were also sucking difficulties and hypothermia. The mother had been taking diazepam (2mg three times a day) on and off for the last three months of her pregnancy, prescribed by her obstetrician because of premature labour during her previous pregnancy. On the twelfth day the child's serum diazepam was still high and the concentration of the active metabolite desmethyldiazepam was even higher. The mother's serum also still contained a high level of diazepam and her breast milk also contained a significant amount of diazepam or metabolites.

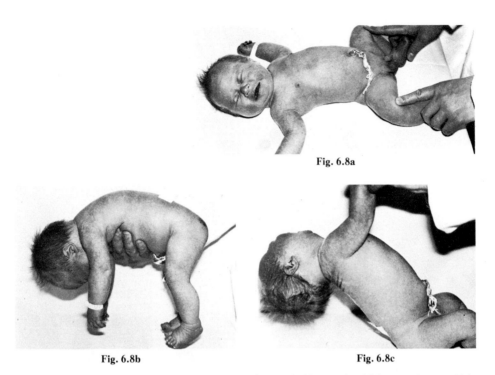

Fig. 6.8a

Fig. 6.8b   Fig. 6.8c

Fig. 6.8. Newborn infant with Down's syndrome, showing marked hypotonia with increased range of joint movement *(a)* and poor posture of trunk, head and limbs in ventral suspension *(b)* and supine *(c)*.

Chromosomal disorders: Down's syndrome (mongolism, trisomy 21)

Hypotonia and delay in achieving motor milestones are constant features of Down's syndrome. The diagnosis is usually obvious on clinical grounds and can be confirmed by chromosomal analysis. The hypotonia is often marked at birth (Fig. 6.8) and tends to persist for a considerable time (Fig. 6.9). There may be a tendency for the tone to improve as motor ability improves, but even after the child is able to stand and walk the tone is often still diminished, and there also appears to be laxity of joint ligaments (Fig. 6.10).

Interesting therapeutic possibilities were raised by Bazelon *et al.* (1967) while studying the effects of 5-hydroxytryptophan on the intellectual capacity of children with Down's syndrome. Although the intellectual state showed no consistent change, there was a striking improvement of the muscle tone. This raised the interesting question as to whether 5-hydroxytryptamine, a product of 5-hydroxytryptophan, had an important rôle to play in the control of muscle tone, not only in infants with Down's syndrome but also in floppy infants generally. However, completion of their studies showed that there was no consistent benefit to children with Down's syndrome from this approach to treatment.

Other trisomic syndromes, *e.g.* trisomy 18, may be associated with increased tone rather than hypotonia. Perhaps the chromosome 21 carries the genetic control of some of the enzyme systems associated with collagen metabolism.

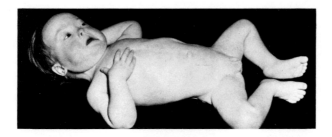

Fig. 6.9a

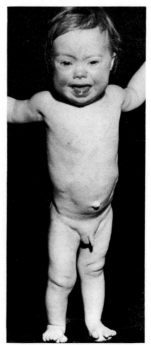

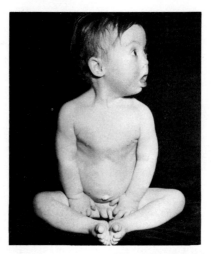

Fig. 6.9c

Fig. 6.9b

Fig. 6.9. 18-month-old child with Down's syndrome showing persistence of hypotonia, with 'frog' posture in supine *(a)*: able to sit without support *(b)* but not to stand unaided *(c)*.

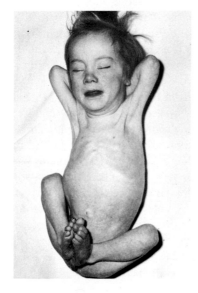

Fig. 6.10. Five-year-old boy with Down's syndrome: persistent hypotonia and increased laxity of joints.

Metabolic disorders

In 1973, Bickel was already able to list more than 40 inborn errors of metabolism with associated brain damage, and the number will undoubtedly continue to increase as more metabolic abnormalities are identified. These cover a wide range of disorders, involving many different pathways of amino acid, carbohydrate, lipid, mucopolysaccharide and protein metabolism, and also deficits in relation to vitamins, hormones, electrolytes, trace elements and other chemicals. Most of these conditions are extremely rare and even the more common ones have an incidence of perhaps one in 2-3000 births. The manifestation of central nervous system involvement usually includes mental retardation, and the additional associated features are very varied. Some of the syndromes may be associated with a significant degree of hypotonia, which in occasional instances may be the main presenting feature, together with delay in reaching motor and other developmental milestones.

Some of the disorders may present at birth or within the neonatal period: in others the symptoms are delayed until much later. The time of onset and the pattern of progression of the features is often fairly consistent in a particular syndrome, and a carefully documented history is of great value in deciding on the appropriate bio-chemical investigations, rather than adopting a 'shot-gun' screening approach by using a wide variety of unnecessary biochemical tests.

Most of the inborn errors of metabolism are inherited by an autosomal recessive mechanism, but a few are X-linked, including Lesch-Nyhan's syndrome, Lowe's syndrome (oculo-cerebro-renal disease), Hunter's syndrome (mucopolysaccharidosis II), Menkes' ('kinky hair') syndrome, and a recently recognized new disorder, also associated with copper metabolism (Haas *et al.* 1980).

Abnormalities of amino acid metabolism

Mental retardation and other central nervous manifestations, such as con-vulsions, are common features in the disorders associated with abnormalities of amino acid metabolism, *e.g.* phenylketonuria. There may be delay in reaching motor milestones, and hypotonia may be present, but these are usually incidental features of less significance. In some disorders, however, motor disability and hypotonia may be striking.

Hyperlysinaemia. Woody (1964) documented a 4½-year-old child with hyper-lysinaemia who apparently had been normal during the first seven months, but had then developed convulsions and subsequently was delayed in mental and motor milestones, with hypotonia and laxity of joint ligaments. He postulated that the laxity of the ligaments and the flabbiness of the muscles might be associated with an impairment in the utilisation of lysine in collagen synthesis. Woody *et al.* (1966) subsequently reported a further follow-up of this case, who was able to walk by the age of three years and apparently had normal motor function at seven years, although still mentally retarded. On screening the family, they found hyperlysinaemia in a 26-month-old sibling and in an 11-year-old cousin of the index case, both of whom appeared to be normal and symptom-free. Metabolic studies revealed an inability to degrade lysine, but Woody and colleagues were unable to pinpoint a specific block or enzyme deficiency. In the light of the two symptom-free cases, they drew attention to the possible pitfalls in assuming a causal relationship if a metabolic abnormality is found when screening patients with mental retardation or associated symptoms.

The two cases of hyperlysinaemia reported by Ghadimi *et al.* (1965) were discovered by screening patients in a mental institution. One, a male aged 27 years, had gross mental as well as physical retardation, was unable to stand or walk, and had hypotonia of the muscles and laxity of the ligaments. The second, a boy of two years, was unable to keep his head erect, to sit or to creep, and was said to have the motor ability of a four-week-old infant.

Non-ketotic hyperglycinaemia. This condition was first recognized by Mabry and Karam (1963) in two infants from the same sibship who presented in the neonatal period with severe neurological distress, hypotonia, repeated convulsions and mental retardation. It is characterized by the development within the newborn period, after an initial symptom-free period of some 18 to 72 hours, of severe hypotonia and lethargy, recurrent convulsions and associated respiratory distress which may need assisted ventilation. Other features include startle reaction, myoclonic jerks and unresponsiveness to painful stimuli. About 30 per cent of these infants die within the first three weeks of life, and those who survive have profound psychomotor retardation (Gitzelmann *et al.* 1977, von Wendt *et al.* 1978). Hyperglycinaemia is thought to be due to a specific defect of the glycine-cleavage enzyme system. In addition to the raised level of glycine in the blood and urine, there is also excess glycine in the

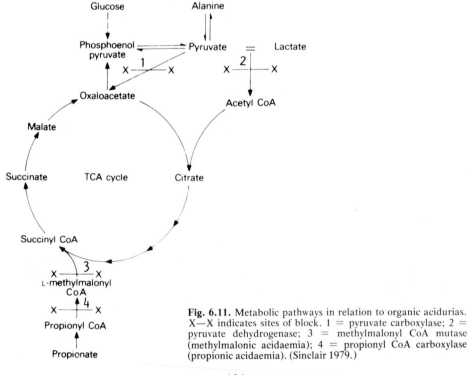

Fig. 6.11. Metabolic pathways in relation to organic acidurias. X—X indicates sites of block. 1 = pyruvate carboxylase; 2 = pyruvate dehydrogenase; 3 = methylmalonyl CoA mutase (methylmalonic acidaemia); 4 = propionyl CoA carboxylase (propionic acidaemia). (Sinclair 1979.)

cerebrospinal fluid and a high glycine level has been demonstrated in postmortem brain tissue. Dalla Bernardina *et al.* (1979) have recently documented four personal cases and reviewed 61 from the literature, and suggested the title 'glycine encephalopathy' to distinguish it from other forms of hyperglycinaemia. In each of their four cases, one or more siblings had previously died in the neonatal period with a similar illness.

Numerous attempts at dietary treatment have failed to influence the course of the disease, in spite of lowering the blood glycine level. A possible therapeutic response to strychnine (a glycine receptor antagonist) was noted by Gitzelmann *et al.* (1977), but the long-term effects are not yet known.

Organic acidaemias/organic acidurias

This rare group of metabolic disorders is characterized by the presence of excess organic acids in the blood and urine as a result of specific metabolic blocks. The metabolic pathways particularly involved are those surrounding the metabolism of pyruvate or those along the pathway from propionate to succinate (Fig. 6.11).

The disorders with an excessive accumulation of pyruvate and lactate fall into two main groups.

In the first group are those in which there is a defect in the complicated and interdependent enzyme systems responsible for pyruvate decarboxylase and dehydrogenase activity in the liver. These include Leigh's encephalomyelopathy, which usually has its onset during the latter part of the first year of life with anorexia and vomiting, and with various neurological signs, including hypotonia and locomotor disability, and disorders of respiration. The course tends to be chronic and slow.

The second main group consists of disorders in the pathway from propionate leading into the tricarboxylic acid cycle via succinate. These include methylmalonic acidaemia and propionic acidaemia, both of which are likely to present in the early newborn period.

Methylmalonic acidaemia was first recognized by Oberholzer *et al.* (1967) in two infants presenting in the first weeks of life with recurrent vomiting, hypotonia, hepatomegaly and, subsequently, failure to thrive and mental retardation. There was also metabolic acidosis and ketosis. They also developed renal failure. The metabolic block is at the level of conversion of methylmalonyl CoA to succinyl CoA by the enzyme methylmalonyl CoA mutase.

Propionic acidaemia was first described by Hommes *et al.* (1968) in a male infant who presented on the third day of life with hypotonia, areflexia, grunting and hyperventilation. He was found to have severe metabolic acidosis, which was unresponsive to sodium bicarbonate and THAM (tris buffer) and he died two days later. The propionic acid level in his blood was 1000 times the normal. The authors postulated that the enzymatic block would be propionyl CoA carboxylase deficiency.

Early diagnosis of these disorders is essential, as the institution of a reduced protein intake can have a dramatic effect on the child's wellbeing and subsequent course (Fig. 6.12). In addition, some of the subtypes of methylmalonic acidaemia may be responsive to vitamin B_{12}.

Often there is also an excess of glycine, hence the original term 'ketotic hyper-

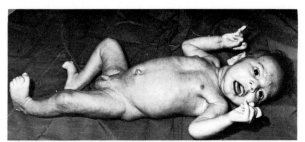

Fig. 6.12a

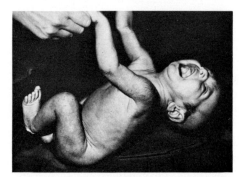

Fig. 6.12b

Fig. 6.12c

Fig. 6.12. Propionic acidaemia. First child of healthy, unrelated Indian parents. Normal for first five days of life. Breast-fed for two days, then changed to artificial milk feeds. On day five began vomiting, became drowsy and dehydrated and lost weight. From day seven developed recurrent twitching and became extremely hypotonic. On day 10 developed respiratory distress followed by apnoea and need for artificial ventilation on day 11. Transferred to neonatal unit at Hammersmith Hospital. Clinical diagnosis of organic acidaemia was confirmed by presence of marked metabolic acidosis with ketosis and hyperglycinaemia, and grossly elevated levels of propionate. He was treated with synthetic diet of restricted protein (2 g/day) plus biotin 5 mg b.d. and vitamin supplements. After stormy neonatal course he steadily improved and by six weeks of age there was dramatic change in tone, although he was still hypotonic *(a, b, c)*. He continued to progress reasonably, but remained somewhat retarded in motor and intellectual milestones. By eight months he was able to sit with support and reached out for objects but had poor hand co-ordination. He had recurrent metabolic and clinical setbacks associated with recurrent infections (mainly respiratory) and he died at 10 months of age.

glycinaemia' for propionic acidaemia. Ugarte *et al.* (1980) have shown that both propionate and methylmalonate inhibit the transport of glycine across the mito-chondrial membrane, which would explain the high glycine level in these conditions. As glycine is an inhibitory neurotransmitter, it may be a contributory factor in the neurological symptoms.

Some organic acidaemias may present at a later age. Hypotonia is a prominent feature in β-hydroxyisovaleric acidaemia with β-methylcrotonyl glycinuria, due to deficiency of β-methylcrotonyl coenzyme A, an enzyme in the degradative pathway of leucine (Stokke *et al.* 1972). This enzyme is biotin-dependent and a good therapeutic response may be obtained from treatment with biotin in *massive* doses (Fig. 6.13) (Keeton and Moosa 1976). A similar case with good response to biotin has recently been reported by Charles *et al.* (1979).

108

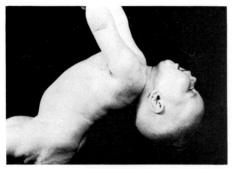 

Fig. 6.13a   Fig. 6.13b

Fig. 6.13. Organic acidaemia/β hydroxyisovaleric acidaemia with β methyl crotonly glycinuira. There were no neonatal problems and development was normal until five months, when she developed upper respiratory infection, treated with ampicillin and cotrimoxazole. Persistent tachypnoea was noted by the parents. Feeds were changed from Cow and Gate V formula to Baby Milk 2 (which has a higher protein content, ratio approximately 3 g/100 ml compared with 1.8 g/100 ml of Cow and Gate). At age eight months she was admitted to a local hospital for investigation of persistent tachypnoea. She also had regression of motor and intellectual development, a very floppy head and did not reach out for toys. Negative results were obtained from investigations of arterial gases, routine blood count, chest X-ray, skull X-ray, barium swallow, Mantoux, bronchoscopy, laryngoscopy, ECG, U and E, calcium, phosphate, sugar, urine aminoacids, viral titres, bacteriology, CSF and skin tests. Precipitins against micropolyspora faeni and avian protein (father keeps pigeons). She was started on prednisolone 20 mg daily but continued to deteriorate steadily and one month later was transferred to the Brompton Hospital for lung biopsy, where it was decided that this was not primarily a respiratory problem but probably neuromuscular, in view of the hypotonia, and she was transferred to Hammersmith Hospital. She had persistent, rapid, deep acidotic respirations with some associated stridor, and was markedly hypotonic, lying in a 'frog' posture, and had marked head lag in supine traction *(a)*. There were some rolling eye movements, she was uninterested in her surroundings and not focusing. She moved very little and appeared to be weak, with very little anti-gravity movement. Tendon reflexes were all brisk and there was unsustained ankle clonus. Tentative diagnosis of organic acidaemia was made, supported by raised blood lactate (4.4. mmol/l, n < 2 mmol) and pyruvate (0.24 mmol/l, n < 0.20); urinary gas chromatography for organic acids showed excess of betamethyl crotonic and betahydroxyisovaleric acids, confirmed by mass spectrometry. Diagnosis of betamethyl crotonyl CoA carboxylase deficiency was made: because this is a biotin sensitive enzyme she was started on treatment with high dosage biotin, 10 mg initially, followed by 5 mg b.d. and the steroids were tailed off. The following morning she was markedly improved, more alert, more mobile, with improved tone, and respiration was strikingly less noisy. After one week there had been further marked improvement and photographic records show difference in head control and posture *(b)*. Six weeks later, aged 11 months, she was smiling and alert, babbling with two clearly recognizable words, sitting unsupported, had normal tone and no weakness, was playing with toys, and her motor performance was around the seven-month level.

Miscellaneous rare metabolic disorders with marked hypotonia

Hypotonia is a consistent feature of many of the rare metabolic disorders affecting the nervous system. The following are some specific examples.

Infantile type of neuronal ceroid lipofuscinosis. This is characterized by normal development in the first year of life and rapid psychomotor retardation from 12 to 18 months of age onwards. Additional features are marked muscle hypotonia, ataxia, visual degeneration and microcephaly, followed later by myoclonic jerks, hyper-excitability and attacks of opisthotonos. Half the cases also develop convulsions. By age three they become blind and bed-bound and they usually die between 8 and 11 years of age. The pathogenesis is thought to be associated with an inborn error of arachidonic acid metabolism (Santavuori *et al.* 1974, Svennerholm *et al.* 1975).

Mulibrey nanism—nanism with *mu*scle, *li*ver, *br*ain and *eye* involvement. This condition is characterized by growth failure from birth, an unusual triangular-shaped face, suggestive of a hydrocephalic facial appearance, a dolicocephalic head and marked hypotonia. The voice is squeaky and the tongue and other oropharyngeal structures are underdeveloped. One of the hallmarks of the condition is the characteristic finding in the ocular fundi of yellowish dots and pigment dispersion in the periphery. There is also a constrictive pericardial fibrosis, which may cause death from congestive cardiac failure. Hypotonia is a common feature in the disease. The inheritance is autosomal recessive, but no metabolic abnormality has yet been identified (Perheentupa *et al.* 1973, 1975).

Muscle, eye and brain disease. The characteristics of this condition are severe early muscle weakness, mental retardation and pathological eye findings, usually with congenital myopia. There are marked feeding and sucking difficulties and general muscle hypotonia from birth. The muscle features include severe early hypotonia in all cases, and retarded motor development, diminished or absent deep tendon

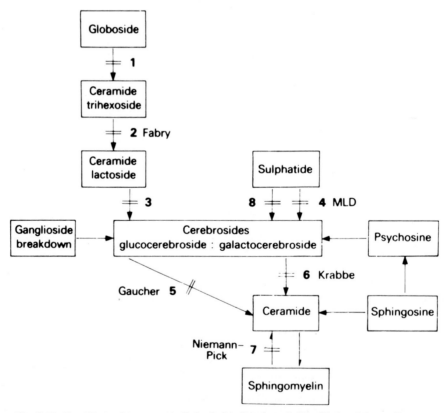

Fig. 6.14. Simplified guide to metabolic basis for disorders of globoside breakdown. Enzymes identified as deficient include 1, N-acetylhexosaminidase; 2, ceramide trihexosidase; 3, galactosidase; 4, arylsulphatases A, B, C; steroid sulphatase; 5, glucocerebrosidase; 6, galactocerebroside β-galactosidase; 7, sphingomyelinase; 8, cerebroside sulphatide sulphotransferase. (Sinclair 1979, p. 290.)

reflexes, a myopathic EMG, elevated creatine phosphokinase and histological findings of muscular dystrophy are invariably present (see also section on congenital muscular dystrophy, p. 82). The eye features include visual failure, congenital myopia, glaucoma and hypoplasia of the optic disc and retina. Brain involvement comprises severe mental retardation, hydrocephalus (during the first year only), myoclonic jerks and/or convulsions, abnormal EEG in childhood, and associated slight spasticity. Of the 14 cases reviewed by Santavuori *et al.* (1977), only one was ambulant and the remainder were severely affected. The condition is inherited as an autosomal recessive. No biochemical abnormality has been recognized.

Cerebro-hepato-renal syndrome (Zellweger's disease). A rare familial disease, this is characterized by severe hypotonia, convulsions, mental retardation and hepatic cirrhosis. The onset of symptoms is usually within the first two years of life and there is rapid progression. Hepatic dysfunction may occur at any time in the course of the illness. The metabolic defect is still unknown, but the demonstration of a raised level of serum pipecolic acid suggests it may be related to hyperpipecolatemia (Gatfield *et al.* 1968, Danks *et al.* 1975, Trijbels *et al.* 1979). This is of some interest in relation to the hypotonia, in view of the metabolic link between pipecolic acid and lysine, and the occurrence of marked hypotonia in hyperlysinaemia and the importance of lysine in the crosslinking of collagen.

Oculo-cerebro-renal syndrome (Lowe's syndrome). This is a rare X-linked disorder, characterized by severe mental retardation, muscular hypoplasia and hypotonia, congenital glaucoma or cataract, renal tubular acidosis, rickets and a generalized aminoaciduria (Lowe *et al.* 1952, Richards *et al.* 1965). The fundamental defect is unknown, but is thought to be an abnormality in membrane transport. Urinary levels of lysine are relatively higher than those of other amino acids, and defective uptake of lysine and arginine by the intestinal mucosa has been demonstrated in two patients by Bartsocas *et al.* (1969).

The sphingolipidoses

This group of rare storage disorders is characterized by the accumulation of sphingolipids in cells of the nervous system, as well as in the reticuloendothelial system and other tissues. Sphingolipids are normally found in cell membranes and have in common a substance called ceramide. They can conveniently be divided into two groups of compounds, globoside and its derivatives and the gangliosides (Figs. 6.14 and 6.15).

Usually the disorders are suspected clinically because of the progressive deterioration in mental function, and individual syndromes are recognized by the associated neurological and visceral features. Hypotonia and motor disability are an incidental feature of a number of these disorders.

Over the years a formidable list of eponymous disorders has accumulated, but with the remarkable advances in understanding of the biochemical basis of these disorders a more holistic and rational approach to diagnosis and classification has been possible. Following the pioneering biochemical studies of Jatzkewitz (1966), Austin (1966) and Cumings (1970), the whole metabolic map in relation to the

111

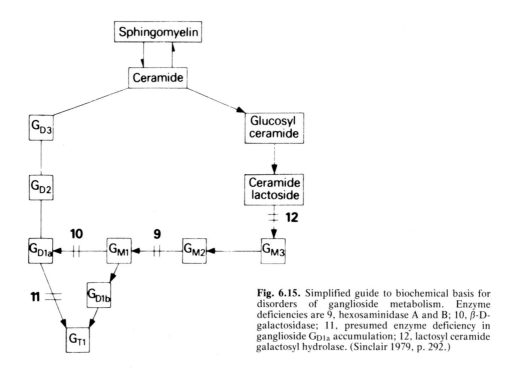

Fig. 6.15. Simplified guide to biochemical basis for disorders of ganglioside metabolism. Enzyme deficiencies are 9, hexosaminidase A and B; 10, β-D-galactosidase; 11, presumed enzyme deficiency in ganglioside G_{D1a} accumulation; 12, lactosyl ceramide galactosyl hydrolase. (Sinclair 1979, p. 292.)

TABLE 6.I

Lipid storage disorders—stored material and enzymatic defect

Disease	Accumulated lipid	Enzyme defect
Gaucher	glucocerebroside	glucocerebroside-β-glucosidase
Niemann-Pick	sphingomyelin	sphingomyelinase
Krabbe	galactocerebroside	galactocerebroside-β-galactosidase
Metachromatic leucodystrophy	sulphatide	arylsulphatase A
Fabry	ceramide trihexoside	ceramide trihexosidase
Tay-Sachs Types I, III, IV, V	GM_2 ganglioside	hexosaminidase A
Tay-Sachs Type II (Sandhoff)	GM_2 ganglioside globoside dermatan and oligosaccharide residues	hexosaminidase A and B
Generalised GM_1	GM_1 ganglioside keratan and oligosaccharide residues	β-galactosidase
Fucosidosis	H-antigen plus glycoprotein residues	α-fucosidase
Ceramide lactoside lipidosis	ceramide lactoside	ceramide lactoside-β-galactosidase
GM_3 hematoside sphingolipidystrophy	GM_3 hematoside	GM_3-UDP-N-acetylgalactosaminyl transferase
Wolman disease	cholesterol esters, triglycerides	undefined acid hydrolases
Cerebrotendinous xanthomatosis	cholestanol	unknown

From: Nausieda and Klawans (1977).

sphingolipidoses has gradually unfolded and the specific enzyme involved in most of the disorders has now been identified (Table 6.I).

Brady (1972) defined five constant biochemical features typifying the sphingo-lipidoses:

(1) in all of these disorders there is an accumulation of a complex lipid in various tissues of the body;

(2) each stored lipid contains ceramide (N-fatty acid-sphingosine);

(3) the rate of synthesis of the stored lipid in patients with these disorders is comparable to that in uninvolved humans;

(4) the enzyme defect in each of these diseases is a deficiency of a specific hydro-lytic enzyme required for the degradation of the accumulating lipid;

(5) the degree of attenuation of enzymatic activity is similar in all of the tissues of an affected individual.

Some lysosomal enzyme systems are related to more than one catabolic pathway, which explains on a biochemical basis the overlap between some of the mucopoly-saccharidoses, representing inborn errors of glycoprotein metabolism, and some of the gangliosidoses, representing glycolipid storage disorders.

Clinically the individual syndromes are recognized on the basis of their fairly consistent features, and confirmation is made on the basis of specific biochemical studies (Fig. 6.16). In those with associated hypotonia and delay in reaching motor milestones, muscle power usually will be proportionately good, but there should be evidence of delay in intellectual milestones, or deterioration in intellectual function.

Some of the lipidoses, such as metachromatic leucodystrophy and Krabbe's globoid cell leucodystrophy, also affect the peripheral nerves (Hagberg *et al.* 1962, Fullerton 1964, Sourander and Olsson 1968, Gamstorp 1968) and thus are readily identified by the marked impairment in motor nerve conduction velocity in the peripheral nerve. Sural nerve biopsy, although not essential for diagnosis, will show

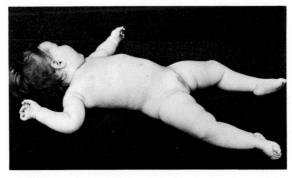

Fig. 6.16. Tay-Sachs disease—GM$_2$ gangliosidosis. 17-month-old girl admitted for investigation of severe hypotonia and head lag from age of five to six months. Inability to sit unsupported and poor vision noted by parents. Up to six months her development apparently had been normal. On examination she was found to be generally hypotonic with very poor head control and inability to maintain sitting posture. She was also relatively immobile and had difficulty in sustaining her arms or legs against gravity. Tendon reflexes were all present. She had exaggerated startle response to noise. Fundi showed classical cherry-red spots in macular region bilaterally. Diagnosis of Tay-Sachs disease confirmed by absence of hexosaminidase A in leucocytes.

demyelinating changes, and also evidence of metachromatic material in meta-chromatic leucodystrophy.

Muscle biopsy is not usually contributory to the diagnosis or identification of this group of disorders. Those with an associated peripheral neuropathy may show evidence of mild denervation changes; those with mainly central involvement usually will show essentially normal muscle, both histologically and histochemically, although there may be some secondary changes in relation to the distribution of individual fibre types. In some instances, however, electronmicroscopy may reveal unusual structural changes, which are probably associated with terminal nerves in the muscle rather than with the muscle fibres themselves (Tomé and Fardeau 1976).

CHAPTER 7

Connective Tissue Disorders

McKusick (1972) has classified a number of syndromes as 'heritable disorders of connective tissue'. These include Marfan's syndrome, Ehlers-Danlos syndrome, osteogenesis imperfecta, the mucopolysaccharidoses and various other genetically determined disorders of bone and supportive tissues. Many of these conditions may be associated with marked laxity of joints and with hypotonia and delay in reaching motor milestones. In general such conditions as the mucopolysaccharidoses are readily recognized clinically by their other presenting features.

Recent advances in knowledge of the structure and synthesis of collagen, and in techniques for collagen analysis, have led to further insight into the molecular basis of various collagen defects. This in turn has brought in its wake further sub-classification of some of the collagen disorders; some seven different types of Ehlers-Danlos syndrome are now postulated. In some forms there is a deficiency in synthesis of a specific collagen type (*e.g.* collagen type 3 deficiency in EDS type IV), whereas in others an enzyme connected with collagen metabolism is deficient (*e.g.* lysyl oxidase, lysyl hydroxylase, pro-collagen peptidase).

In a recent review, McKusick (1976) suggested dividing the heritable disorders of connective tissue into those involving predominantly the fibrous elements and those which are disorders of mucopolysaccharide degradation (Table 7.1, p. 123). The defects in the synthesis and cross-linking of fibrous elements could be further classified into *(a)* those with an apparent primary disorder of the biochemical machinery for synthesis of connective fibres and *(b)* those metabolic disorders which cause secondary damage to the connective tissue as a result of accumulated metabolites or by other mechanisms.

Laxity of joint ligaments may also occur as an isolated phenomenon, often with a familial tendency, and in practice this is probably the most common connective tissue disorder in relation to the floppy infant (Fig. 7.1).

Congenital laxity of ligaments

Increased mobility of joints associated with hypotonia of the muscle has been recognized for a long time (Finkelstein 1916, Sobel 1926, Key 1927, Sturkie 1941). Cases are often familial and inheritance appears to be by a dominant mechanism. There is no intellectual impairment and motor power and reflexes are normal. It is probably a common condition and usually is asymptomatic. Carter and Wilkinson (1964) observed excessive mobility in at least four pairs of joints in 7 per cent of 285 schoolchildren, while Sutro (1947) found three or more pairs of joints to be hypermobile in 4 per cent of 435 adult orthopaedic patients.

Children with laxity of ligaments and joint hypermobility may present with congenital dislocation of the hips, with delayed motor milestones and hypotonia in infancy (Fig. 7.2), with progressive scoliosis (Figs. 7.2, 7.3) or with 'clumsiness' or more obscure symptoms (Fig. 7.4). The following manoeuvres are worth documenting in order to make an objective assessment of joint laxity and hypermobility:

(1) increased mobility of wrist and thumb, with approximation of thumb to anterior aspect of forearm;

(2) hyperextension of metacarpophalangeal joints of fingers, with extension of wrist to 90°;

(3) hyperextension of elbows beyond 180°;

(4) hyperextension of knees beyond 180°;

(5) dorsiflexion of ankles beyond 45° from the neutral position;

(6) increased range of abduction of hips (usually to 90°).

Ehlers-Danlos syndrome

The cardinal features of Ehlers-Danlos syndrome are in the skin, which is excessively stretchable, easily bruised and fragile, and in the joints, which are hyperextensible (Figs. 7.5, 7.6). Some seven different varieties have now been identified on clinical, genetic and biochemical grounds (McKusick 1976, Pope and Nicholls 1978) (Table 7.II). Types I and II are the classical varieties in severe and mild form, type III is the benign hypermobility syndrome (which probably overlaps with isolated joint laxity). All three are inherited as an autosomal dominant trait. Type IV is a malignant disorder, liable to spontaneous rupture of gut or large arteries, and is characterized by a deficiency in synthesis of type III collagen. There are at least two subtypes, and possibly more. Inheritance is autosomal recessive. Type V Ehlers-Danlos is x-linked and not particularly distinctive: it has been associated with lysyl oxidase deficiency. Type VI is autosomal recessive and is characterized, in addition to the usual features, by scoliosis and fragility of the eyeballs. This was the first connective tissue disorder in which a specific enzyme deficiency (lysyl hydroxylase) was identified. Type VII Ehlers-Danlos is also autosomal recessive: characteristically there is profound joint laxity and this type usually presents with bilateral dislocated hips at birth. (The pedantic might like to use the term 'arthrochalasis multiplex congenita'.) It is associated with a deficiency of the enzyme procollagen peptidase (the enzyme responsible for converting procollagen to collagen).

Marfan syndrome

The Marfan syndrome is inherited as an autosomal dominant and may have as much heterogeneity as the Ehlers-Danlos syndrome. The clinically similar syndrome associated with homocystinuria has been separated from it (Carson *et al.* 1965). McKusick (1976) considers the triad of ectopia lentis, long thin extremities and aortic aneurysm as the features most essential for Marfan syndrome. However, any of these features can be absent in a substantial proportion of cases. McKusick has tentatively defined four separate varieties, and more will probably follow (Table 7.III). In the Marfanoid hypermobility syndrome there are associated features of Ehlers-Danlos syndrome, such as loose-jointedness and stretchable skin (Fig. 7.7).

116

Mucopolysaccharidoses

The mucopolysaccharidoses are a rare group of lysosomal storage disorders in which there is an excessive accumulation of acid mucopolysaccharides—particularly dermatan sulphate, heparan sulphate and keratan sulphate—in various tissues and cells, and more especially in cartilage and bone. The clinical features are variable, involving the skeletal system, the eyes, nervous system, liver and spleen and various other organs.

These disorders are usually suspected on clinical presentation and confirmed by appropriate screening and quantitative biochemical assessment of the urine, and by biochemical tests on lymphocytes or cultured fibroblasts. Antenatal diagnosis is now possible in a number of them by biochemical estimation of amniotic fluid or culture of amniotic fibroblasts.

There has been considerable advance over the past 10 years in the biochemical designation of the specific syndromes; for details see the excellent reviews by McKusick (1972, 1976), McKusick *et al.* (1978) and Sinclair (1979).

These infants may present with marked hypotonia and delay in motor and intellectual development, but the diagnosis is usually suspected clinically because of the facial appearance and other features, such as corneal opacities, stunted growth, kyphosis and abnormalities on radiography of the vertebrae or hands, *stiff* joints and abnormalities of the heart valves.

Thus the majority of these cases will present with neurological, ocular, growth or general problems (Table 7.IV) but for some, as in the type IV mucopolysaccharidosis (Morquio-Brailsford syndrome), the main features are the skeletal deformities, the laxity of ligaments and delay in motor development, so these cases may present predominantly with hypotonia or problems in ambulation (Fig. 7.8).

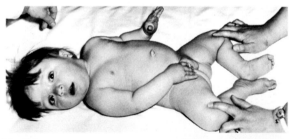

Fig. 7.1a

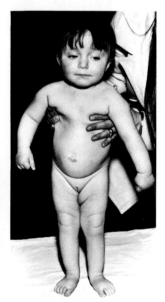

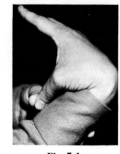

Fig. 7.1. One-year-old child who had been noted at birth to have dislocation of both hips. Good therapeutic results from splinting in abduction until six months, then noted to have residual increased range of hip mobility, which persisted *(a)*. No muscle weakness and able to sustain bodyweight *(b)*. Mother found to be 'double jointed', with increased range of movement in many joints *(c)*, suggesting that dominantly inherited laxity of joint ligaments would account for the dislocated hips.

Fig. 7.1c

Fig. 7.1b

117

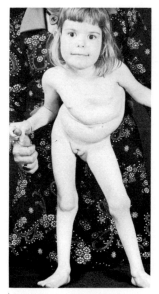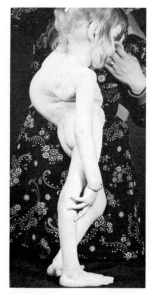

Fig. 7.2. Hypotonia; laxity of ligaments; connective tissue disorder. Four-year-old girl with delayed motor milestones, showing difficulty with gait and progressive scoliosis. She still had difficulty walking unaided. Note extreme degree of scoliosis and associated hyperextension of knees and eversion of feet. Muscle power was normal, as were CPK, EMG and nerve conduction velocity. Scoliosis was very mobile and considerable reduction was achieved with a Milwaukee brace, but almost certainly she will need spinal fusion later. This severe deformity should be preventable if diagnosed and treated early in its course.

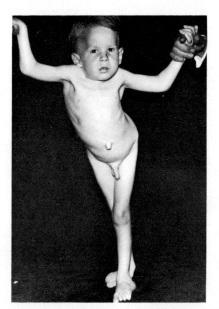

Fig. 7.3. Hypotonia; laxity of ligaments; connective tissue disorder. Four-year-old boy presenting with delay in motor milestones and progressive scoliosis. Note associated calcaneo-valgus deformity and marked mobility of ankles. Muscle power, CPK, nerve conduction and EMG normal. (Note striking resemblance to girl in Fig. 7.2.)

118

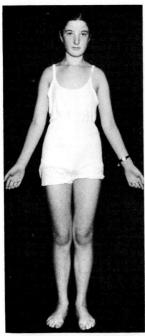

Fig. 7.4a

Fig. 7.4b

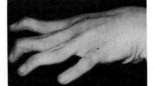

Fig. 7.4c

Fig. 7.4d

Fig. 7.4. Congenital laxity of ligaments. Nine-year-old girl *(a)* had difficulty with turning locks and doorknobs. No associated weakness. Found to have increased range of movement in various joints *(b, c, d)*. In infancy there had been delay in motor milestones; she was unable to sit up until nine months or to walk unsupported until four years. When younger she sat in odd postures and was able to do 'the splits'.

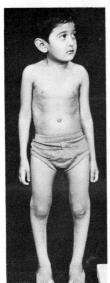

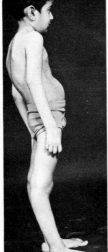

Fig. 7.5a, b

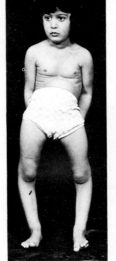

Fig. 7.5c, d

Fig. 7.5. Ehlers Danlos syndrome. 4½-year-old boy *(a, b)* and his 3½-year-old sister *(c, d)*, presenting with delay in motor milestones and abnormality of gait. Note marked joint mobility, with hyperextension of knees, bowing of legs and kyphosis *(continued on next page)*.

119

| Fig. 7.5e | Fig. 7.5f |

(**Fig. 7.5.** *cont.*)
Other joints, including hands *(e, f)*, also affected. Both children also had parchment-like scars from earlier lacerations. Muscle power good, and CPK, nerve conduction and EMG normal.

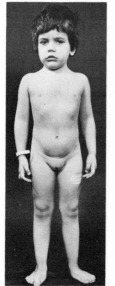

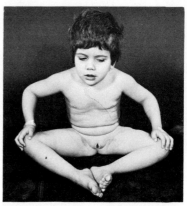

Fig. 7.6c

Fig. 7.6a

Fig. 7.6b

Fig. 7.6. Ehlers Danlos syndrome/joint mobility. Three-year-old girl with delay in motor milestones and increased joint mobility *(a, b, c)*. Note valgus and everted posture of feet and slight hyperextension of knees. She walked with support at 15 months but without support only at two years. She also had bilateral CDH. There was slightly excessive elasticity of the skin. Her father has striking hyperelasticity of skin *(d, e)* and increased joint mobility *(f)*. Probably Ehlers Danlos Type 3.

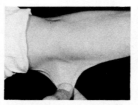

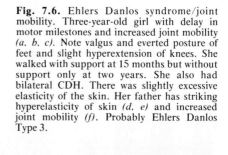

| Fig. 7.6d | Fig. 7.6e | Fig. 7.6f |

120

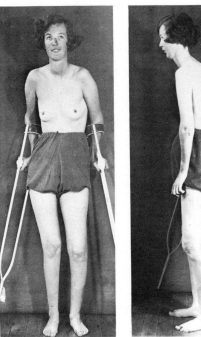

Fig. 7.7a   Fig. 7.7b

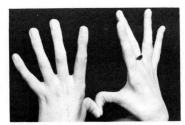

Fig. 7.7c

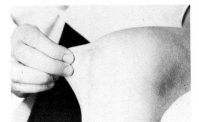

Fig. 7.7d

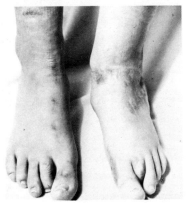

Fig. 7.7e

Fig. 7.7. 'Marfanoid hypermobility syndrome'. 20-year-old girl who had been born by breech delivery with bilateral talipes equinovalgus deformity. There had been marked delay in motor milestones; she was unable to maintain a sitting posture until 21 months, to stand with support until three years, and to walk unaided until past four years. She remained hypotonic, with increased joint mobility, and had poor circulation in the legs, with coldness and cyanosis below the knees. She had frequent bruising and purpura and a tendency to skin laceration after mild trauma, which healed poorly. At 20 years she was 70-inches tall (178 cm) and still hypotonic *(a, b)*, with hyperextensible joints *(c)* and readily dislocatable patellae. Skin showed hyperelasticity *(d)* and many 'tissue-paper' scars *(e)*. She also had high-arched palate, arachnodactyly and non-toxic diffuse goitre. Her three brothers and their children were all normal on examination, but one brother was tall (75 inches). Her mother had bilateral Dupuytrens contractures of all four fingers. This patient presents a combination of features of Marfan and Ehlers-Danlos syndromes, but has no abnormality of eyes or aorta.

121

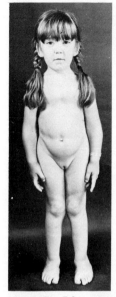

Fig. 7.8a   Fig. 7.8b

For caption see facing page.

Fig. 7.8c

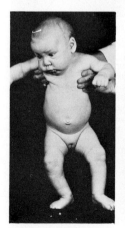
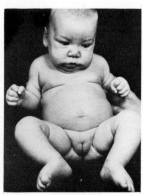

Fig. 7.8d   Fig. 7.8e   Fig. 7.8f

122

Fig. 7.8. Mucopolysaccharidosis type IV (Morquio-Brailsford syndrome). Five-year-old girl referred because of gait abnormality. Motor milestones had been normal but she developed marked pes planus and genu valgum *(a, b)*. She was short in stature and had chest deformity, dorsal kyphosis and increased joint mobility, particularly in wrists, which had marked ulnar deviation *(c)*. Clinical diagnosis of type IV MPS was supported by wrist X-ray showing absence of end of ulna, and of vertebral bodies showing typical 'fish-mouth' shape, and confirmed by presence of keratan sulphate in urine. Her intellect was normal and there were no ocular or cardiac abnormalities. On follow-up she remained very stunted in growth and her skeletal deformities progressed, tending to recur following corrective orthopaedic procedures. In a subsequent pregnancy (despite genetic counselling about the autosomal recessive risk) her mother refused amniocentesis and antenatal diagnosis. The female sibling appeared to be normal at birth but had a similar facies to her sister. Diagnosis of MPS IV was made in the neonatal period on excess keratan sulphate in her urine. Intellectual and early motor milestones were normal and at three months she was sitting with support and taking weight on her legs *(d, e)*. She subsequently developed the same wrist, vertebral and skeletal deformities, as well as strikingly similar facial appearance, stature and chest deformity, as her sister (*f*, aged two years).

TABLE 7.I

Biochemical classification of heritable disorders of connective tissue (McKusick 1976)

(1) *Defect in synthesis and cross-linking of fibrous elements*

    (a) Primary: Ehlers-Danlos syndrome
                      Osteogenesis imperfecta
                      ? Marfan syndrome

    (b) Secondary: Alkaptonuria
                      Homocystinuria
                      Menkes syndrome

(2) *Defects in mucopolysaccharide degradation*

      (a) Single enzyme deficiencies: mucopolysaccharidoses I, II, IIIA, IIIB, (IV), VI, VII

      (b) Multiple hydrolase deficiencies: mucolipidoses II and III

TABLE 7.II
Classification of Ehlers-Danlos syndrome (EDS)

Type	Name	Classical features	Inheritance	Chemical defect
I	EDS gravis	Classical severe	Autosomal dominant	Type I collagen substitution?
II	EDS mitis	Classical mild	Autosomal dominant	Unknown
III	EDS benign hypermobile	Joint hypermobility	Autosomal dominant	Unknown
IV	EDS ecchymotic acrogeria	Lethal arterial rupture	Autosomal recessive	Deficiency type III collagen
V	EDS X-linked	Mild classical	Sex linked	Lysyl oxidase deficient
VI	EDS (ocular form)	Retinal detachment, scoliosis	Autosomal recessive	Lysyl hydroxylase deficient
VII	EDS (arthrochalasis multiplex)	Severe joint laxity, shortness	Autosomal recessive	Procollagen peptidase deficient

From: Pope and Nicholls (1978).

TABLE 7.III
Varieties of Marfan syndrome (McKusick 1976)

Asthenic form
Non-asthenic or Lincolnesque form
Marfanoid hypermobility syndrome
Contractural arachnodactyly

TABLE 7.IV

Classification of the mucopolysaccharidoses (MPS) and mucolipidoses (ML)

	Type	Eponym	Clinical features				Urinary MPS			Enzyme defect
			Neurological signs	Dwarfism	Corneal clouding	Cardiovascular involvement	HS	DS	KS	
MPS	I H	Hurler	Marked	Marked	Severe	Marked	+	+		α-L-iduronidase
MPS	I S	Scheie	None	Mild	Severe	Late	+	+		α-L-iduronidase
MPS	II	Hunter	Mild to moderate	Marked	Absent (? late)	Late	+	+		Iduronosulphate sulphatase
MPS	III	Sanfilippo A, B	Marked	Moderate	Absent	Rare	+			A. Heparan N-sulphatase B. α-N-acetylglucosaminidase
MPS	IV	Morquio	None	Marked	Late	Late			+	Hexosamine-6-sulphatase
MPS	V	Vacant								
MPS	VI	Maroteaux-Lamy	None	Marked	Severe	Present		+		Aryl sulphatase B
MPS	VII		Variable: none to severe retardation, macroencephaly	Marked	Variable	Present	+	+		β-glucuronidase
ML	II	I-cell disease	Severe	Marked	Present	Present				Multiple lysosomal hydrolase deficiency
ML	III	pseudo-Hurler	Mild	Marked	Present	Aortic valves				As for ML II

Key to symbols: HS = heparan sulphate; DS = dermatan sulphate; KS = keratan sulphate.
Adapted from Menkes (1980) and McKusick (1976).

CHAPTER 8

Miscellaneous

Prader-Willi syndrome (hypotonia-obesity syndrome)

This unusual syndrome was originally recognized by Prader *et al.* (1956), who described five males and four females with adiposity, short stature, mental sub-normality, undescended testes in the males, and a history of marked hypotonia and feeding difficulty in the newborn period. Motor milestones were delayed, but the hypotonia gradually decreased. The obesity developed at about two years of age. Prader and Willi (1963) subsequently reviewed 14 cases (eight male and six female) and pointed out the consistency of the clinical features.

The syndrome usually presents with profound hypotonia at birth and with feeding difficulty necessitating tube feeding. The infant's birthweight is frequently below 3000g at term. There is a characteristic facies, with a high forehead, dolicho-cephalic head, small almond-shaped eyes and an open triangular-shaped mouth. The hair is usually very fair and the eyes are blue. (However, in one Indian and one Cape Coloured child I have seen, the complexion and hair have been dark and the eyes not blue.) The hands and feet are small.

The hypotonia gradually improves and eventually these children pass various motor milestones and achieve the ability to walk, usually after the age of two years.

There is a tendency to gross generalized obesity, which usually develops after the child starts walking, but in some cases this occurs earlier. Diet control is very difficult, and hyperphagia is very difficult to handle in the older children.

Growth is stunted, the majority being below the 50th percentile; bone age is also retarded.

The males usually have undescended testes and a rudimentary scrotum, but do develop secondary sex characteristics. The testes are present intra-abdominally.

There is intellectual impairment, the IQ usually falling in the 40 to 80 range. The deficit in intelligence is often less striking in early infancy than later.

Diabetes of the adult type tends to develop in adolescence and an abnormal glucose tolerance curve may be obtained in childhood on standard testing with steroid provocation.

Extensive chromosome, metabolic and endocrinological investigations have failed to reveal any consistent abnormality in this syndrome. With only occasional exceptions, the vast majority of cases recorded have been isolated, so a genetic basis appears to be unlikely. However, there is suggestive evidence of a defect of genetic material relating to the short arm of the No. 15 chromosome in Prader-Willi syndrome and some 10 per cent of all cases have cytological evidence of imbalance of chromatin from this chromosome. These include 15:15 translocation (Fraccaro *et al.* 1977) and an unbalanced 15:3 translocation detectable from trypsin banding (Kucerova *et al.* 1979). In a recent detailed study of endocrine function in five male and three female cases of Prader-Willi syndrome Jeffcoate *et al.* (1980) concluded that the hypogonadism was due to combined hypothalamic and primary gonadal abnormalities.

Serum enzymes, nerve conduction velocity, electromyography and muscle biopsy studies are essentially normal. A few reports on minor histological changes probably reflect secondary changes in muscle rather than a primary muscle involvement.

The higher incidence of males in the literature probably reflects the more ready diagnosis because of undescended testes. A typical male and a typical female case, showing the marked facial resemblance and consistent pattern of the disease, are illustrated in Figs. 8.1 and 8.2.

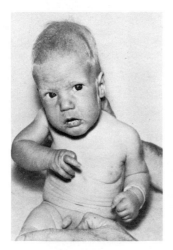 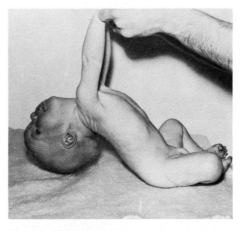

Figs. 8.1a *(left)*, **8.1b** *(right)*

 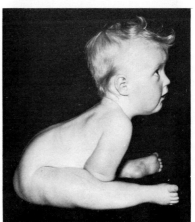

Figs. 8.1c *(left)*, **8.1d** *(right)*
For caption see page 129

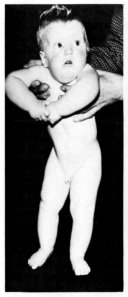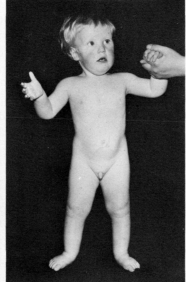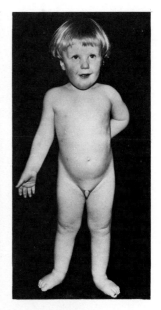

Fig. 8.1e   **Figs. 8.1f** *(left)*, **8.1g** *(right)*

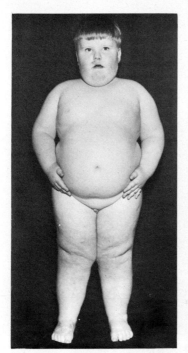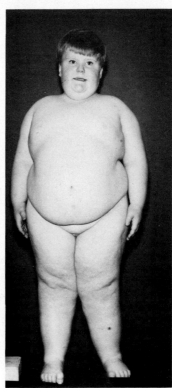

Figs. 8.1h *(above)*, **8.1i** *(right)*

For caption see next page

128

Fig. 8.1. Prader-Willi syndrome. This infant was born at home, three weeks prematurely, with birthweight of 2490g. During pregnancy, fetal movements were often absent for up to three days. He was admitted to hospital at 2½ hours with hypothermia (93°F, 34°C), profound hypotonia and immobility. He was unable to suck or swallow and had very weak cry. Moro and grasp reflexes and all tendon jerks were absent. Fair-haired and blue-eyed, he had unusual facies with high forehead, dolicocephalic-shaped head, small almond-shaped palpebral fissures and small triangular-shaped mouth *(a)*. Penis was small, scrotum rudimentary and both testes undescended. At two weeks he was still grossly hypotonic, with severe head lag, but there were spontaneous limb movements. Initially, diagnosis of 'benign congenital hypotonia' was made. By five weeks, limb movements improved further and he was able to suck, but still needed tube feeding. He first smiled at nine weeks. Knee jerks could first be elicited at 13 weeks and all tendon reflexes were present by eight months. At four months he had some head control when supported in sitting position *(a)* but still marked head lag in supine *(b)*. He subsequently showed a steady improvement and by seven months was able to sit with support *(c)*. At 11 months he was sitting without support *(d)* and was also able to stand supported *(e)*. He was standing well and walking with one hand held by 20 months *(f)* and was able to walk unaided by 26 months *(g)*. His weight remained below the third centile from birth to about 30 weeks, after which it rose to about the 80th centile by one year and remained at that level till about three years, when it increased precipitously and by five years had reached 42 kg, which was more than twice the 90th centile for this age *(h)*. Height, in contrast, remained just below the 50th centile. Bone age was consistently retarded, and at five years was at about a two-year level. Despite attempts at dietary restriction his weight continued to rise *(i, aged 6½ years)*. Early intellectual development seemed reasonable and retardation seemed predominantly motor, but later he showed unequivocal delay in intellectual milestones and his intelligence quotient was found to be about 60. During a respiratory infection at 17 months he had two convulsions lasting about five minutes each. He had three further short convulsions at three years of age. Chromosome karyotype and glucose tolerance tests were normal. He died unexpectedly at home, aged eight years.

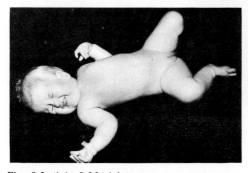
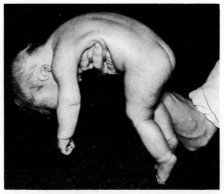

Figs. 8.2a *(left)*, **8.2b** *(right)*

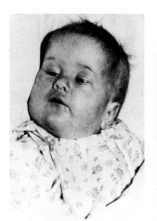
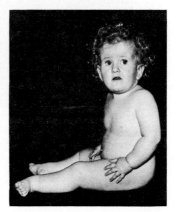

Figs. 8.2c *(left)*, **8.2d** *(right)*

For caption see page 131

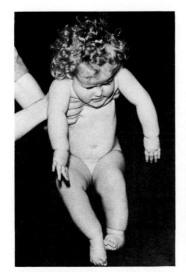

Fig. 8.2e

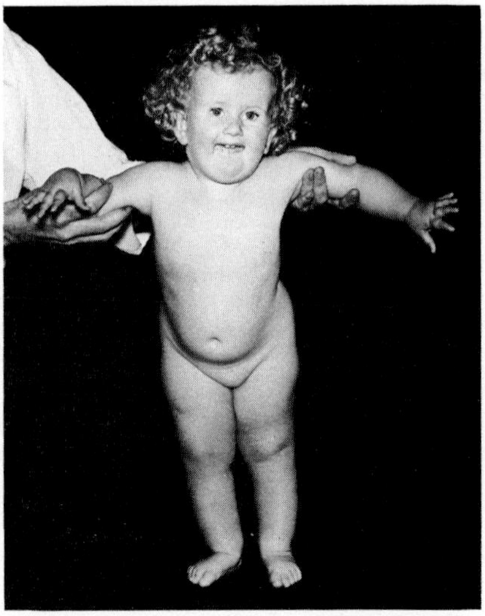

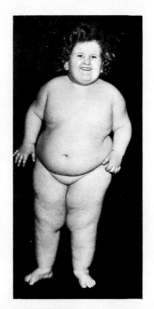

Fig. 8.2f

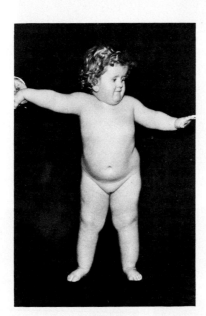

Fig. 8.2g

Fig. 8.2h

For caption see facing page

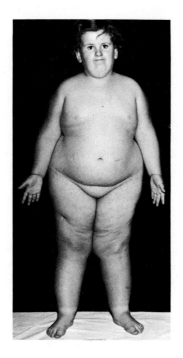
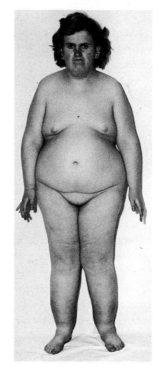

Figs. 8.2i *(above)*, **8.2j** *(right)*

Fig. 8.2. Prader-Willi syndrome. This girl was born by caesarean section at 36 weeks following a diagnosis of mild diabetes in the mother. Birthweight was 3430g. She was very hypotonic at birth, slow to cry and was unable to suck or swallow. Facies and dolicocephalic head *(a)* were strikingly similar to previous case (Fig. 8.1). At six weeks she was still fed by tube (gavage) and had generalised hypotonia *(b)* but good spontaneous limb movements *(c)*. Knee and ankle jerks were easily elicited, but other tendon jerks were absent. By 10 weeks she was sucking normally, starting to smile, and taking an interest in her surroundings. At 15 weeks she could raise her head in prone. There was gradual improvement and by nine months she was sitting with support, and by one year unsupported. At 15 months she was sitting quite steadily *(d)* but was still unable to support her weight standing *(e)*. She was standing with support by 19 months *(f)* and at 2½ years was walking with one hand held *(g)*. She did not walk without support till 3½ years *(h)*. At six months she had several short episodes of unconsciousness suggestive of convulsions but these did not recur. Her weight remained around the 50th centile until two years but then rose precipitously *(g. h)* and by four years four months *(h)* was almost double the 90th centile at 34.5 kg. Her height, in contrast, was at the 10th centile and her bone age at a two-year level. Weight continued to increase despite advice and efforts at dietary restriction, which was very difficult to enforce (*i*, aged eight years; *j*, aged 15 years). Initial intellectual development seemed reasonable and by 15 months she had a good vocabulary of simple words and good manipulative (motor) skills. However, she later had retardation of intellectual development and, despite speaking in full sentences, her comprehension was below normal and she experienced difficulty at school. Glucose tolerance curve was normal (at five years) and chromosome karyotype was normal, apart from an abnormality in the No. 16 chromosome which was also present in her mother and considered to be a marker chromosome.

Metabolic, nutritional and endocrine disorders

As already mentioned, hypotonia may be an incidental feature of many metabolic, nutritional and endocrine disorders in infancy. In a number of these hypotonia may be a relatively insignificant feature of the disease, but in some it may be the presenting feature.

Metabolic

Among the metabolic disorders, infantile hypercalcaemia and renal tubular acidosis may be associated with marked hypotonia. Correction of the underlying disorder will usually result in improvement of the hypotonia. The child may often present with failure to thrive, and diagnosis will depend on recognition of the biochemical disorder.

Nutritional

Hypotonia is an almost constant feature of rickets and usually responds to therapy with vitamin D (Fig. 8.3). In some cases of severe rickets the hypotonia and apparent associated weakness may be so profound, together with indrawing of the rib cage with respiration, as to suggest a clinical diagnosis of Werdnig-Hoffmann disease.

Children with coeliac disease often have associated hypotonia, which at times may be the most striking and presenting feature (Fig. 8.4). It usually resolves as the child responds to a gluten-free diet.

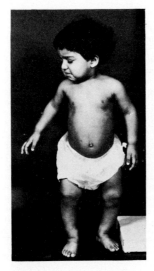 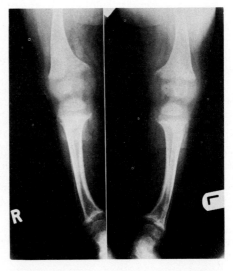

Fig. 8.3. Rickets. Two-year-old child presenting with bowing of legs, abnormal gait and associated hypotonia. Note prominence of wrists and lower femoral epiphyses, *(left)*. X-ray of legs showed typical epiphysial changes, *(right)*.

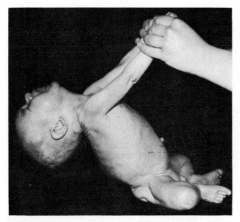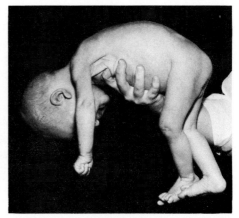

Fig. 8.4. Coeliac disease. 21-week-old child with failure to thrive from age 16 weeks and marked hypotonia, with poor head control but good muscle power. Note prominent abdomen and wasted buttocks.

Endocrine

In cretinism or Cushing's syndrome the underlying diagnosis will usually be suspected because of the characteristic signs (Fig. 8.5), but hypotonia may be an associated feature. In infantile hypothyroidism there is a marked slowing of motor nerve conduction velocity (Moosa and Dubowitz 1971).

Congenital heart disease

All standard texts mention hypotonia in association with congenital heart disease, but in practice the association is exceptional. One wonders whether both the hypotonia and the congenital heart lesions are more likely to be coincidental manifestations of a more generalized disorder (Fig. 8.6). The two may certainly be associated in Marfan's syndrome and mongolism, and type 2 glycogenosis (Pompe's disease) affects cardiac as well as skeletal muscle.

The first case on record of hypotonia in association with congenital heart disease is the four-year-old girl described by Davison and Weiss (1929). In addition to her extreme flaccidity and cyanotic congenital heart lesion, she also had exophthalmos, unilateral ptosis and external rectus weakness, suggesting a more extensive condition.

'Benign congenital hypotonia' ('Essential hypotonia')

I have placed this diagnosis at the end because it is a shrinking entity, if indeed it is an entity at all. I think that in time it may well disappear from our nomenclature.

If the term is to be retained, it should not be used in as broad a sense as Walton (1956) suggested. His cases of 'benign congenital hypotonia' with residual muscular weakness and disability probably included examples of the mild form of spinal muscular atrophy or of non-progressive congenital myopathies, which need specialized techniques for recognition of the lesion in the muscle.

If the term is to be used at all, it is best confined to those cases which on clinical grounds have marked hypotonia with no associated weakness, no delay in other developmental milestones, no associated disease and with a tendency to improve.

Even these cases of benign hypotonia may in time be recognized as merely symptomatic of some associated disorder. Connective tissue disorders with laxity of joint ligaments and supportive tissues, and disorders such as Prader-Willi syndrome, have to be carefully excluded.

However, one does still see the occasional floppy infant with no associated muscle weakness and no disorder in other systems, who has a delay in motor milestones but who is eventually completely normal (Figs. 8.7-8.9). For this infant a diagnosis of 'benign congenital hypotonia' still seems completely appropriate.

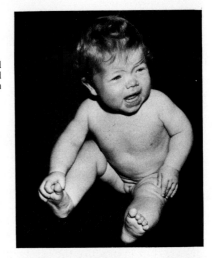

Fig. 8.5. Hypothyroidism. 16-month-old child presenting with delay in motor and intellectual milestones and with hypotonia.

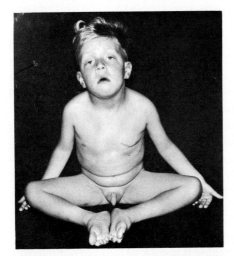

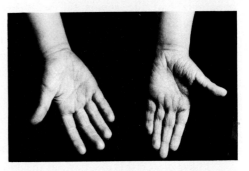

Fig. 8.6. Congenital heart disease. This child was born with cyanotic congenital heart disease and diagnosis of Fallot's tetralogy was later confirmed by catheterization. During pregnancy fetal movements had been less than in pregnancies of his three older siblings. He was floppy as an infant and all motor milestones were delayed. He only sat unsupported at two years, stood after four years and walked at 4½ years, three months after a pulmonary valvotomy. When I did his cardiac catheterization at the age of 3 years 11 months I was struck not only by his general hypotonia and lax joints but also by elasticity of his skin and saphenous vein, which easily admitted a size 7 cardiac angiographic catheter and would probably have accommodated two. He had an associated ptosis, bilateral simian creases and unusual pattern of palmar and plantar creases reminiscent of Down's syndrome. Chromosome karyotype was normal; intelligence was probably low normal. Family history was negative for muscle, joint or heart problems. Associated joint and skin manifestations suggest connective tissue disorder.

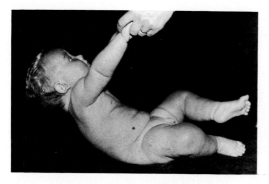

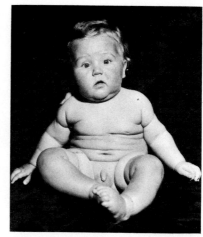

Fig. 8.7a *(above)*, **8.7b** *(right)*

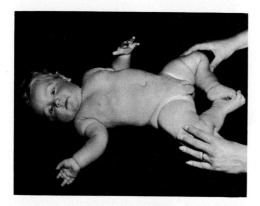

Fig. 8.7c *(above)*, **8.7d** *(right)*

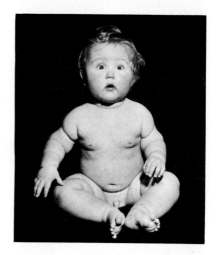

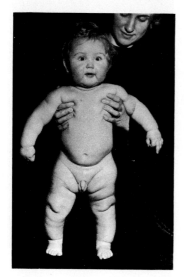

Fig. 8.7e

Fig. 8.7. Benign congenital hypotonia. This male infant was born at term following normal delivery and weighed 3740g. Hypotonia of trunk and limbs and marked head lag in supine were noted in the newborn period. There was no apparent weakness and tendon reflexes were present. At 3½ months he was still hypotonic, with head lag, but was improving. By five months he had no head lag in supine *(a)* and was able to sit with support *(b)* but was still hypotonic, and hips still abducted readily to 90° *(c)*. By one year he was sitting well without support *(d)*, pivoting and taking his weight on his legs *(e)*. Intellectual development was normal. He walked unaided by 15 months and had no residual motor deficit.

135

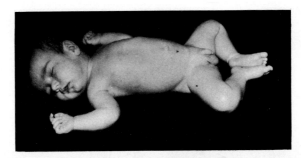

Fig. 8.8a

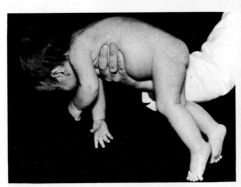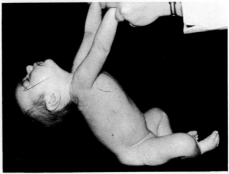

Figs. 8.8b *(left)*, **8.8c** *(right)*
For caption see facing page

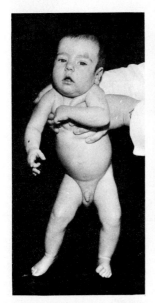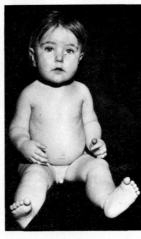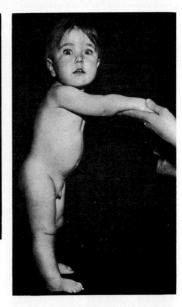

Figs. 8.8d *(left)*, **8.8e** *(above)*,
8.8f *(right)*

136

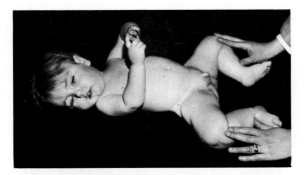

Fig. 8.8g

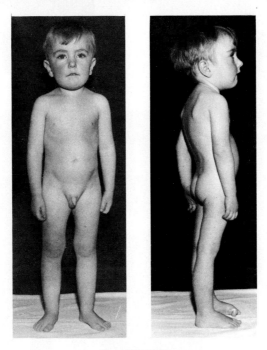

Figs. 8.8h, 8.8i

Fig. 8.8. Benign congenital hypotonia. This infant, born at term after a normal delivery, was noted to be hypotonic from the newborn period and at three months still had 'frog' posture with full hip abduction *(a)*, poor posture in ventral suspension *(b)*, head lag in supine *(c)* and was unable to support his bodyweight *(d)*. There was good anti-gravity movement of limbs; nerve conduction and EMG were normal. He steadily improved and by 13 months was sitting well without support *(e)*, was able to stand with support *(f)* but still had increased range of hip abduction *(g)*. He walked unaided by two years and by three seemed normal in motor function *(h)*, although still ungainly in running and 'clumsy' in various motor activities. He had poor posture, with abdomen protuberance, lumbar lordosis and thoracic kyphosis *(i)*.

137

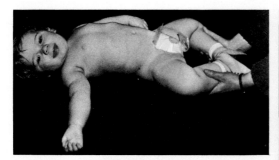

Fig. 8.9a

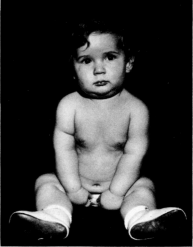

Fig. 8.9b

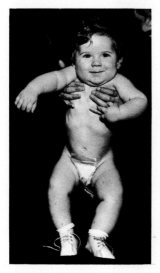

Fig. 8.9c

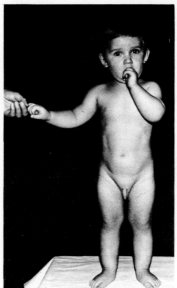

Figs. 8.9d *(left)*, **8.9e** *(right)*

Fig. 8.9. Benign congenital hypotonia. This bright little child presented at nine months with hypotonia and delay in motor milestones *(a)*. He was able to sit well without support *(b)* but unable to take his weight standing *(c)*. CPK, nerve conduction and EMG were normal. He subsequently showed steady improvement and was able to stand unsupported and to start walking by 20 months *(d. e)*. He had no residual disability.

CHAPTER 9

Diagnostic Procedures

The sequence in which various diagnostic procedures are done will be determined by the provisional clinical assessment of the floppy infant (Fig. 9.1). In the paralytic group, these investigations will be directed at establishing the presence and nature of any underlying neuromuscular disorder, and the definitive investigation is the muscle biopsy. In the non-paralytic group, the possibilities are much broader and investigations must be tailored to the particular clinical entity which is diagnosed. For this reason it is important to establish a provisional clinical diagnosis in the first place and then to do the appropriate (rather than inappropriate) investigations.

Associated clinical features

The presence of associated clinical features in combination with hypotonia may be helpful in the differential diagnosis. The following is a list of some of the more important causes in relation to various associated features.

Hypotonia with associated sucking/swallowing difficulty in the newborn period

There are a number of conditions in which feeding difficulty may be a specific

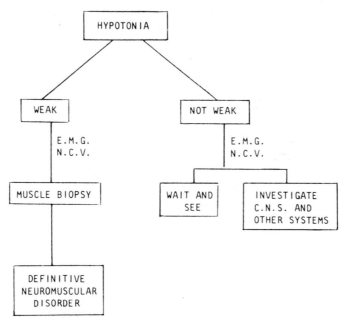

Fig. 9.1. A clinical approach to the classification of the floppy infant.

problem in the immediate newborn period in addition to hypotonia. These include:

Severe infantile spinal muscular atrophy. This is the result of associated bulbar palsy due to involvement of the lower cranial nerves. There is accumulation of mucus in the throat. The facial muscles are not affected.

Congenital myotonic dystrophy. Marked feeding difficulty is a common manifestation of the congenital form of myotonic dystrophy. The problem is probably already present *in utero* since there is often a history of hydramnios. There is a tendency to gradual improvement and subsequent resolution of the swallowing difficulty within two to three months after birth. There is invariably an associated involvement of the face, with bilateral facial weakness and a characteristic facies with a tent-shaped mouth (see Chapter 5). Since myotonia is not a feature of these infants, one cannot readily explain the swallowing difficulty on the basis of myotonia of the striated muscle of the pharynx. Possibly it is associated with the severe hypotonia, which is also transitory and may be due to an additional factor, possibly of an immunological nature from the mother which crosses the placenta.

Prader-Willi syndrome. Feeding difficulty is a concomitant feature of the Prader-Willi syndrome. It tends to resolve within the first six or eight weeks of life. There is no associated facial weakness. The generalized hypotonia is often profound and the infant may appear to be motionless in the first few days of life.

Myasthenia gravis. Transitory neonatal myasthenia in the newborn infant of a myasthenic mother, as well as congenital infantile myasthenia, may present as a floppy infant with associated bulbar weakness. Sometimes there are acute choking episodes as a presenting symptom.

Birth trauma. Feeding difficulties may be a sequel in infants with central nervous system involvement following trauma or hypoxia in the perinatal period. There are usually other signs of cerebral or pyramidal tract involvement.

Hypotonia with associated facial weakness

The presence of facial weakness in association with a weak, floppy infant should raise the possibility of one of the following conditions:
  (1) congenital myotonic dystrophy;
  (2) myotubular myopathy;
  (3) myasthenia gravis;
  (4) congenital muscular dystrophy.

Hypotonia with associated external ophthalmoplegia

This is particularly seen in the following conditions:
  (1) mitochondrial myopathy ('ophthalmoplegia plus' syndrome);
  (2) myotubular myopathy;
  (3) myasthenia gravis;
  (4) congenital dystrophia myotonica.

Hypotonia with 'arthrogryposis'

Arthrogryposis or 'bent joints', with muscle contractures and limited range of joint movements, results from immobility of the infant *in utero* and may be associated

140

with neuromuscular disorders or be secondary to intra-uterine factors such as bicornuate uterus or oligohydramnios in Potter's syndrome, or following amniocentesis. In some cases there may be associated swallowing difficulty. The neuromuscular disorders most likely to be associated with severe deformity at birth are:

(1) congenital muscular dystrophy;
(2) congenital myotonic dystrophy;
(3) denervation syndromes.

In spite of the fact that many joints are rigid and relatively immobile, other joints may have increased range of movement and associated hypotonia of the muscles and there is frequently an associated congenital dislocation of the hips in relation to the syndrome.

Three main lines of investigation are of value in the diagnosis of neuromuscular disorders—electrodiagnosis, serum enzymes and muscle biopsy.

Electrodiagnosis

This is a very useful *routine* technique for trying to identify or exclude a neuro-muscular disorder in the floppy infant. The two basic tests are nerve conduction velocity and electromyography. Nerve conduction velocities should always be done first as they do not involve the use of needles and thus are not likely to upset the child and make further tests difficult.

As a preliminary to any procedure, the confidence of the child should be obtained. Usually the procedure can be done with the child on the parent's lap and he should be engaged in some activity, such as looking at a picture book or playing with some toy, in order to distract his attention from the actual procedure itself.

Nerve conduction velocity

Motor nerve conduction velocity is easily measured by stimulating the nerve with surface electrodes at two appropriate points along its course. The response is recorded by a further surface electrode over an appropriate distal muscle, and the difference in latency following the two separate stimuli, divided by the length of nerve between the stimulating electrodes, gives the nerve conduction velocity.

A very marked slowing, to about half the normal velocity or less, suggests a demyelinating peripheral neuropathy. In neuronal or axonal neuropathies the velocity may be at the lower limit of normal or slightly below the normal range. Conduction velocity is also slowed in infantile spinal muscular atrophy, and the action potential is very small, especially in the legs (Moosa and Dubowitz 1976).

Sensory nerve conduction velocities are more difficult to elicit and require more refined equipment. In general we have found that this additional procedure is unnecessary as routine and we have reserved it for those cases in whom we have actually obtained a reduction in motor nerve conduction velocity or in those where there has been overt evidence of sensory deficit.

Electromyography

Although an EMG in a six-month-old infant may seem a formidable undertaking to a neurologist or electrophysiologist used to dealing with adults who obey his instructions, for the paediatrician or electrophysiologist used to handling infants and children this is a fairly simple and rapid procedure, and one that should be included as a routine screening procedure for all floppy infants as part of the initial clinical assessment. In the neuromuscular group it will help to confirm the presence of a disorder and also to define its nature whereas in the non-paralytic group it may reveal neuropathy in association with a central nervous system disorder.

One should decide in advance which muscle is going to provide most information; as a routine we use either the quadriceps in the leg or the deltoid in the arm. Other accessible muscles can also be used. In general it should not be necessary to sample more than one muscle.

Needles should be inserted rapidly and are usually readily accepted by the child. One should go right into the muscle with one neat stroke and not move around too much initially. The needle can then gradually be withdrawn until an optimal place within the muscle is found with a good response.

Initially the muscle is completely relaxed and extended by placing the corresponding joint (the knee or shoulder) in the appropriate position. Normally there is complete silence at rest and the gain on the machine should be increased appropriately (to say $50\mu V/div$) to see whether any spontaneous spike waves can be picked up at rest, which would imply a denervation process. The examiner then encourages the child to move the limb, either by starting this passively or by stroking the foot or using an alternative procedure to produce some withdrawal. Recordings are taken at minimal, moderate and maximal effort and attempts made to assess both the interference pattern and its extent. The basic characteristics of the electromyogram are as follows.

Normal. The individual waves are normally bi-phasic or tri-phasic and of an amplitude between $300\mu V$ and 5mV. With full volition there is a full interference pattern, which is recognized by the fact that the baseline between individual waves disappears and there is a continuous activity.

Myopathic. In myopathies of any kind the basic changes are that the waves become polyphasic, and there is a reduction in the amplitude of the individual waves (usually less than 1mV). There is normal interference, so no baseline is visible between the potentials. There is complete silence at rest, as in the normal muscle.

Denervation. Positive sharp waves are obtained at rest. These can usually be heard on the amplifier as short 'pips' and are recognized as positive spike waves on the tracing. With volition, there is a diminished interference pattern and lengths of the baseline are visible between the potentials. This is due to fall-off in active motor units as a result of the denervating process. In addition there are either isolated, individual small spike waves or large polyphasic potentials (fasciculation potentials), which imply a reinnervation process with abnormally large motor units. These large polyphasic units are usually found in conditions with anterior horn cell involvement, such as spinal muscular atrophy.

The electromyogram should give one the following basic information: (1) is the tracing normal or abnormal? (2) if it is abnormal, is it of a neurogenic or a myopathic type?

The procedure should be looked on merely as a *screening* technique; it will not give any further information as to the type of myopathy or the type of denervation.

There are two additional disorders which can be recognized on electrodiagnostic tests, myotonia and myasthenia.

Myotonia. This is a spontaneous burst of activity of 100/sec or more, with a gradual decrement. On the acoustic amplification it is readily recognized as a 'dive-bomber' sound, or akin to the sound of a motor cycle taking off at speed and disappearing into the distance. Myotonic bursts can be provoked in a patient by tapping on the muscle, and also as 'insertional activity' when inserting the needle, so it is useful to have the acoustic connection on at the time the needle is inserted.

Myotonia should be sought not only in proximal muscles but also in small distal muscles, such as the interossei, when dystrophia myotonica is suspected. In floppy infants with congenital myotonic dystrophy, myotonia may be absent in the early stages and the diagnosis can be verified more readily by examination of the mother, who will usually show at least minimal clinical evidence of myotonia and overt myotonic bursts on EMG.

'Pseudomyotonia' is not true myotonia but spontaneous bursts of activity which sound similar to myotonia. It is found in various types of myopathy, but more consistently in type II glycogenosis and may be a clue to diagnosis of that condition. There is usually no decrement with the bursts of activity and the waves tend to be of similar amplitude.

Myotonia is not observed in hypothyroidism, and the so-called 'myotonic jerks' with delayed relaxation of the tendon reflexes do not represent myotonia. Myotonia may also be an associated feature in the hyperkalaemic form of periodic paralysis.

Myasthenia. Myasthenia can be demonstrated by the fatiguability of muscle on repetitive stimulation of the nerve. The procedure can be uncomfortable, so the duration of stimulation should be relatively short (say 0.05msec). Supramaximal stimulation is given at a frequency of 20/sec for up to one minute. The characteristic picture is a decrement in the amplitude of the wave with repetitive stimulation, which is a reflection of the fatiguability of the muscle. In some patients presenting with fairly focal involvement, such as that of the ocular muscles only or involving proximal muscles, one may get a negative result when assessing the distal muscles of the arm, so the result should not be taken to exclude the diagnosis of myasthenia. If the clinical picture points strongly to myasthenia, a therapeutic trial with neostigmine is often worth doing if the edrophonium intravenous test is also initially negative.

Serum enzymes

Creatine phosphokinase (CPK) is the enzyme most widely studied in the diagnosis of muscle disease. It is grossly elevated in muscular dystrophies and other degenerative muscle disorders but tends to be normal or sometimes only moderately elevated in denervating conditions. CPK is of comparatively little value in relation to the floppy infant syndrome, as it tends to be normal in the vast majority of congenital myopathies, the neurogenic disorders and the hypotonias associated with the non-paralytic group of disorders. It is invariably normal in severe infantile spinal muscular atrophy, but may be slightly or moderately elevated in the milder variants. It is raised in congenital muscular dystrophy, but unlike the very gross elevation in Duchenne dystrophy, it is extremely variable and may range from within normal limits to levels of about five to 10 times normal. The occasional case of Duchenne dystrophy presenting with hypotonia and delayed motor milestones in the first year of life usually has CPK in the order of 2000-5000 units, *i.e.* above 10 times the normal levels. (Note that different methods of CPK estimation have different normal ranges.)

An unexplained, consistent elevation of CPK in the absence of overt muscle weakness or hypotonia in a child presenting with a postural deformity such as scoliosis should raise the possibility of malignant hyperpyrexia. Diagnosis is important in view of the danger associated with anaesthesia.

Muscle biopsy
This is the sheet-anchor of diagnosis in the floppy infant syndrome and an essential procedure in the investigation of all floppy infants with associated muscle weakness. The procedure is readily done under local anaesthesia, and in my view a general anaesthetic is not only unnecessary but positively contra-indicated in these infants, who often have respiratory deficit as well. With the advent of needle biopsy the procedure is even less traumatic, requires no incision beyond a small nick in the skin (under local anaesthesia) and no sutures. In general the quadriceps is a readily accessible and satisfactory muscle for biopsy, but in occasional conditions with unusual distribution of weakness another muscle may be selected (*e.g.* deltoid in localized scapulo-humeral weakness).

Once a biopsy is undertaken it is essential that it is properly processed to get the fullest possible information from it, and that it is not promptly destroyed by immersion in formalin (the standard procedure in the past). *Enzyme histochemistry* is an essential part of the routine assessment of every biopsy, as it will ensure the recognition of many of the congenital myopathies that would be completely missed on routine staining. (For further details on biopsy techniques and interpretation see Dubowitz and Brooke 1973, and for correlations with specific clinical syndromes see Dubowitz 1978.) A useful series of stains for routine analysis of a biopsy is given in Table 9.I. These will identify most of the 'structural' congenital myopathies and also some of the metabolic ones; where specific metabolic disorders are suspected, parallel biochemical studies of the appropriate storage product and enzyme deficiencies should be done.

Electronmicroscopy is a useful additional tool in the recognition of some of the congenital myopathies, and particularly some of the ones with abnormalities that are not apparent on light microscopy. As it is a time-consuming procedure, one may have to be selective in its application, but it is worth processing part of the muscle biopsy for electronmicroscopy as a routine in all cases so that sections can be cut as appropriate after the light microscopy studies are completed.

Muscle biopsy is not of much diagnostic value in the non-neuromuscular group of floppy infants although some observations may be made in relation to predominance or selective atrophy of one fibre type, or other non-specific secondary changes. In some of the storage disorders affecting the central nervous system, abnormalities may be detected in muscle biopsy, especially with electronmicroscopy, and presumably relate to affected nerve terminals or other non-muscle elements.

TABLE 9.I

Routine histological and histochemical stains

Stain	*Shows*
Haematoxylin and Eosin	General architecture/pathology
Verhoeff-van Gieson	General architecture/pathology Connective tissue proliferation Nerves
Gomori trichrome	General architecture/pathology Focal structural change in fibres 'Ragged red fibres'
ATPase	Fibre types Selective fibre type changes

NADH-TR	Fibre types
	Structural changes in fibres,
	    e.g. mitochondrial abnormality
	        central cores

Acid phosphatase	Degenerative change
Periodic Acid Schiff (PAS)	Glycogen storage
Oil red O	Lipid storage

Abbreviations: ATPase = adenosine triphosphase; NADH-TR = nicotinamide adenine dinucleotide tetrazolium reductase.

References

Aicardi, J., Conti, D., Goutières, F. (1974) 'Les formes néonatales de la dystrophie myontonique de Steinert.' *Journal of the Neurological Sciences*, **22**, 149-164.

Afifi, A. K., Smith, J. W., Zellweger, H. (1965) 'Congenital non-progressive myopathy. Central core disease and nemaline myopathy in one family.' *Neurology*, **15**, 371-381.

Armstrong, R. M., Koenigsberger, R., Mellinger, J., Lovelace, R. E. (1971) 'Central core disease with congenital hip dislocation: study of two families.' *Neurology*, **21**, 369-376.

Arnon, S. S., Midura, T. F., Damus, K., Thompson, B., Wood, R. M., Chin, J. (1979) 'Honey and other environmental risk factors for infant botulism.' *Journal of Pediatrics*, **94**, 331-336.

Austin, J. H. (1966) 'Recent enzyme studies during life and post-mortem in metachromatic and globoid leukodystrophy.' *In:* Lüthy, F., Bischoff, A. (Eds.) *Proceedings of the 5th International Congress of Neuropathology, Zurich, Sept. 1965, I.C.S. No. 100.* Amsterdam: Excerpta Medica, pp. 426-428.

Aylett, P. (1954) 'Five cases of acute infective polyneuritis (Guillain-Barré syndrome) in children.' *Archives of Disease in Childhood*, **29**, 531-536.

Badurska, B., Fidzianska, A., Kamieniecka, Z., Prot, J., Strugalska, H. (1969) 'Myotubular myopathy.' *Journal of the Neurological Sciences*, **8**, 563-571.

Bank, W. J., di Mauro, S., Bonilla, E., Capuzzi, D. M., Rowland, L. P. (1975) 'A disorder of muscle lipid metabolism and myoglobinuria.' *New England Journal of Medicine*, **292**, 443-449.

Barth, P. G., van Wijngaarden, G. K., Bethlem, J. (1975) 'X-linked myotubular myopathy with fatal neonatal asphyxia.' *Neurology*, **25**, 531-536.

Bartsocas, C. S., Levy, H. L., Crawford, J. D., Thier, S. (1969) 'A defect in intestinal amino acid transport in Lowe's syndrome.' *American Journal of Diseases of Children*, **117**, 93-95.

Baskin, J. L., Soule, E. H., Mills, S. D. (1950) 'Poliomyelitis of the newborn: pathologic changes in two cases.' *American Journal of Diseases of Children*, **80**, 10-21.

Batten, F. E. (1903) 'Three cases of myopathy, infantile type.' *Brain*, **26**, 147-148.

Bazelon, M., Paine, R. S., Cowie, V. A., Hunt, P., Houck, J. C., Mahanand, D. (1967) 'Reversal of hypotonia in infants with Down's syndrome by administration of 5-hydroxytryptophan.' *Lancet*, **1**, 1130-1133.

Beevor, C. E. (1902) 'A case of congenital spinal muscular atrophy (family type) and a case of haemorrhage into the spinal cord at birth giving similar symptoms.' *Brain*, **25**, 85-108.

Bell, D. B., Smith, D. W. (1972) 'Myotonic dystrophy in the neonate.' *Journal of Pediatrics*, **81**, 83-86.

Bethlem, J., van Gool, J., Hulsmann, W. C., Meijer, A. E. F. H. (1966) 'Familial non-progressive myopathy with muscle cramps after exercise: a new disease associated with cores in the muscle fibres.' *Brain*, **89**, 569-588.

—— Meijer, A. E. F. H., Schellens, J. P. M., Vroom, J. J. (1968) 'Centronuclear myopathy.' *European Neurology*, **1**, 325-333.

Bickel, H. (1973) 'The clinical pattern of inborn metabolic errors with brain damage.' *In:* Hommes, F. A., van den Berg, C. J. (Eds.) *Inborn Errors of Metabolism.* London: Academic Press, pp. 15-32.

Black, R. E., Arnon, S. S. (1977) 'Botulism in the United States, 1976.' *Journal of Infectious Diseases*, **136**, 829-832.

Bossen, E. H., Shelburne, J. D., Verkauf, B. S. (1974) 'Respiratory muscle movement in infantile myotonic dystrophy.' *Archives of Pathology*, **97**, 250-252.

Brady, R. O. (1972) 'Enzyme defects in the sphingolipidoses and their application to diagnosis.' *Annals of Clinical and Laboratory Science*, **2**, 285-294.

Brandt, S. (1950) *Werdnig-Hoffmann's Infantile Progressive Muscular Atrophy.* Copenhagen: Munksgaard.

Brooke, M. H. (1973) 'Congenital fiber type disporportion.' *In:* Kakulas, B. A. (Ed.) *Clinical studies in Myology: Proceedings of 2nd International Congress on Muscle Diseases, Perth, Australia, 1971. Part 2, I.C.S. No. 295.* Amsterdam: Excerpta Medica, pp. 147-159.

—— (1977) *A Clinician's View of Neuromuscular Diseases.* Baltimore: Williams & Wilkins.

—— Neville, H. E. (1972) 'Reducing body myopathy.' *Neurology*, **22**, 829-840.

Brown, B. I., Brown, D. H. (1966) 'Lack of an α-1,4-glucan-6-glycosyl transferase in a case of type IV glycogenosis.' *Proceedings of the National Academy of Sciences of the U.S.A. (Washington)*, **56**, 725-729.

—— —— (1968) 'Glycogen-storage diseases. Types I, III, IV, V, VII and unclassified glycogenoses.' *In:* Dickens, F., Randle, P. J., Whelan, W. J. (Eds.) *Carbohydrate Metabolism and its Disorders, Vol. 2.* New York: Academic Press, pp. 123-150.

Bundey, S. (1972) 'A genetic study of infantile and juvenile myasthenia gravis.' *Journal of Neurology, Neurosurgery and Psychiatry*, **35**, 41-51.

Byers, R. K., Banker, B. Q. (1961) 'Infantile muscular atrophy.' *Archives of Neurology*, **5**, 140-164.

—— Taft, L. T. (1957) 'Chronic multiple peripheral neuropathy in childhood.' *Pediatrics*, **20**, 517-537.

Campbell, M. J., Rebeiz, J. J., Walton, J. N. (1969) 'Myotubular, centronuclear or pericentronuclear myopathy?.' *Journal of the Neurological Sciences*, **8**, 425-443.

147

Carson, M. J., Pearson, C. M. (1964) 'Familial hyperkalemic periodic paralysis with myotonic features.' *Journal of Pediatrics*, **64**, 853-865.

Carson, N. A. J., Dent, C. E., Field, C. M., Gaull, G. E. (1965) 'Homocystinuria: clinical and pathological review of ten cases.' *Journal of Pediatrics*, **66**, 565-583.

Carter, C., Wilkinson, J. (1964) 'Persistent joint laxity and congenital dislocation of the hip.' *Journal of Bone and Joint Surgery*, **46B**, 40-45.

Cavanagh, N. P. C., Lake, B. D., McMeniman, P. (1979) 'Congenital fibre type disproportion myopathy: a histological diagnosis with an uncertain clinical outlook.' *Archives of Disease in Childhood*, **54**, 735-743.

Chambers, R., MacDermot, V. (1957) 'Polyneuritis as a cause of "amyotonia congenita".' *Lancet*, **1**, 397-401.

Charles, B. M., Hosking, G., Green, A., Pollitt, R., Bartlett, K., Taitz, L. S. (1979) 'Biotin-responsive alopecia and developmental regression.' *Lancet*, **2**, 118-120.

Collier, J., Wilson, S. A. K. (1908) 'Amyotonia congenita.' *Brain*, **31**, 1-44.

Conen, P. E., Murphy, E. G., Donohue, W. L. (1963) 'Light and electron microscopic studies of "myogranules" in a child with hypotonia and muscle weakness.' *Canadian Medical Association Journal*, **89**, 983-986.

Conomy, J. P., Levinsohn, M., Fanaroff, A. (1975) 'Familial infantile myasthenia gravis: a cause of sudden death in children.' *Journal of Pediatrics*, **87**, 428-430.

Crosby, T. W., Chou, S. M. (1974) ' "Ragged-red" fibres in Leigh's disease.' *Neurology*, **24**, 49-54.

Cumings, J. N. (1970) 'The lipidoses.' *In:* Vinken, P. J., Bruyn, G. W. (Eds.) *Handbook of Clinical Neurology, Vol. 10. Leucodystrophies and Poliodystrophies.* Amsterdam: North Holland, pp. 325-361.

Cunningham, M., Stocks, J. (1978) 'Werdnig-Hoffmann disease: the effects of intrauterine onset on lung growth.' *Archives of Disease in Childhood*, **53**, 921-925.

Dalla Bernardina, B., Aicardi, J., Goutières, F., Plouin, P. (1979) 'Glycine encephalopathy.' *Neuropädiatrie*, **10**, 209-225.

Danks, D. M., Tippett, P., Adams, C., Campbell, P. (1975) 'Cerebro-hepato-renal syndrome of Zellweger: a report of eight cases with comments upon the incidence, the liver lesion, and a fault in pipecolic acid metabolism.' *Journal of Pediatrics*, **86**, 382-387.

Davison, C., Weiss, M. M. (1929) 'Muscular hypotonia associated with congenital heart disease.' *American Journal of Diseases of Children*, **37**, 359-366.

Debré, R., Thieffry, S. (1951) 'Remarques sur le syndrome de Guillain-Barré chez l'enfant (à propos de 32 observations personnelles). *Archives Françaises de Pédiatrie*, **8**, 357-364.

Di Donato, S., Cornelio, F., Balestrini, M. R., Bertagnolio, B., Peluchetti, D. (1978) 'Mitochondria-lipid-glycogen myopathy, hyperlactacidemia and carnitine deficiency.' *Neurology*, **28**, 1110-1116.

Donner, M., Rapola, J., Somer, H. (1975) 'Congenital muscular dystrophy: a clinico-pathological and follow-up study of 15 patients.' *Neuropädiatrie*, **6**, 239-258.

Drachmann, D. A. (1968) 'Ophthalmoplegia plus, the neurodegenerative disorders associated with progressive external ophthalmoplegia.' *Archives of Neurology*, **18**, 654-674.

Dubowitz, L. M. S., Dubowitz, V. (1977) *Gestational Age of the Newborn: A Clinical Manual.* California: Addison-Wesley.

—— —— (1980) *Assessment of Neurological Function in the Newborn Infant. Clinics in Developmental Medicine.* London: S.I.M.P. with Heinemann Medical; Philadelphia: Lippincott *(in preparation).*

—— —— Goldberg, C. (1970) 'Clinical assessment of gestational age in the newborn infant.' *Journal of Pediatrics*, **77**, 1-10.

—— —— Palmer, P., Verghote, M. (1980) 'A new approach to the neurological assessment of the pre-term and full-term newborn infant.' *Brain and Development*, **2**, 3-14.

Dubowitz, V. (1963) 'Problems of muscular hypotonia in infancy.' *In:* Muscular Dystrophy Group (Eds.) *Current Research in Muscular Dystrophy: Proceedings of the 2nd Symposium.* London: Pitman, pp. 34-54.

—— (1964) 'Infantile muscular atrophy. A prospective study with particular reference to a slowly progressive variety.' *Brain*, **87**, 707-718.

—— (1965) 'Intellectual impairment in muscular dystrophy.' *Archives of Disease in Childhood*, **40**, 296-301.

—— (1969) *The Floppy Infant. Clinics in Developmental Medicine No. 31.* London: S.I.M.P. with Heinemann Medical; Philadelphia: Lippincott.

—— (1975) 'Neurological fragility in the newborn: influence of medication in labour.' *British Journal of Anaesthesia*, **47**, 1005-1010.

—— (1978) *Muscle Disorders in Childhood.* Philadelphia: W. B. Saunders.

—— Pearse, A. G. E. (1960a) 'Oxidative enzymes and phosphorylase in central core disease of muscle.' *Lancet*, **2**, 23-24.

—— —— (1960b) 'Reciprocal relationship of phosphorylase and oxidative enzymes in skeletal muscle.' *Nature (London)*, **185**, 701-702.

—— Platts, M. (1965) 'Central core disease of muscle with focal wasting.' *Journal of Neurology, Neurosurgery and Psychiatry*, **28**, 432-437.

—— Roy, S. (1970) 'Central core disease of muscle: clinical, histochemical and electron microscopic studies of an affected mother and child.' *Brain*, **93**, 133-146.

148

Dunn, L. J., Dierker, L. J. (1973) 'Recurrent hydramnios in association with myotonia dystrophica.' *Obstetrics and Gynecology,* **42,** 104-106.

Dyck, P. J., Thomas, P. K., Lambert, E. H. (Eds.) (1975) *Peripheral Neuropathy.* Philadelphia: W. B. Saunders.

Dyken, P. R., Harper, P. S. (1973) 'Congenital dystrophia myotonica.' *Neurology,* **23,** 465-473.

Engel, A. G., Angelini, C. (1973) 'Carnitine deficiency of human skeletal muscle with associated lipid storage myopathy: a new syndrome.' *Science,* **179,** 899-902.

—— —— Gomez, M. R. (1972) 'Fingerprint body myopathy.' *Mayo Clinic Proceedings,* **47,** 377-388.

—— Gomez, M. R., Groover, R. V. (1971) 'Multicore disease.' *Mayo Clinic Proceedings,* **10,** 666-681.

Engel, W. K. (1967) 'A critique of congenital myopathies and other disorders.' *In:* Milhorat, A. T. (Ed.) *Exploratory Concepts in Muscular Dystrophy and Related Disorders. I.C.S. No. 147.* Amsterdam: Excerpta Medica, pp. 27-40.

Engel, W. K., Foster, J. B., Hughes, B. P., Huxley, H. E., Mahler, R. (1961) 'Central core disease: An investigation of a rare muscle cell abnormality.' *Brain,* **84,** 167-185.

—— Wanko, T., Fenichel, G. M. (1964) 'Nemaline myopathy, a second case.' *Archives of Neurology,* **11,** 22-39.

Fardeau, M., Harpey, J-P., Caille, B. (1975) 'Disproportion congénitales des différents types de fibre musculaire avec petitesse relative des fibres de type 1—documents morphologiques concernant les biopsies musculaires prélevées chez trois membres d'une même famille.' *Revue Neurologique,* **131,** 745-766.

Fernandes, J., Huijing, F. (1968) 'Branching enzyme deficiency glycogenosis: studies in therapy.' *Archives of Disease in Childhood,* **43,** 347-352.

—— van de Kamer, J. H. (1968) 'Hexose and protein tolerance tests in children with liver glycogenosis caused by a deficiency of the debranching enzyme system.' *Pediatrics,* **41,** 935-944.

Finkelstein, H. (1916) 'Joint hypotonia with congenital and familial manifestations.' *New York State Journal of Medicine,* **104,** 942-944.

Ford, F. R. (1960) *Diseases of the Nervous System in Infancy, Childhood and Adolescence. 4th edn.* Springfield, Ill.: C. C. Thomas, p. 1259.

Fraccaro, M., Zuffardi, O., Buhler, E. M., Jurik, L. P. (1977) '15/15 translocation in Prader-Willi syndrome.' *Journal of Medical Genetics,* **14,** 275-276.

French, J. H., Sherard, E. S., Lubell, H., Brotz, M., Moore, C. L. (1972) 'Trichopolio-dystrophy. I. Report of a case and biochemical studies.' *Archives of Neurology,* **26,** 229-244.

Fried, K., Pajewski, M., Mundel, G., Caspi, E., Spira, R. (1975) 'Thin ribs in neonatal myotonic dystrophy.' *Clinical Genetics,* **7,** 417-420.

Fukuyama, Y., Kawazura, M., Haruna, H. (1960) 'A peculiar form of congenital progressive muscular dystrophy. Report of 15 cases.' *Pediatria Universitatis Tokyo,* **4,** 5-8.

Fullerton, P. M. (1964) 'Peripheral nerve conduction in metachromatic leucodystrophy (sulphatide lipidosis).' *Journal of Neurology, Neurosurgery and Psychiatry,* **27,** 100-105.

Gamstorp, I. (1956) 'Adynamia episodica hereditaria.' *Acta Paediatrica (Uppsala),* Suppl. **108,** 1-126.

—— (1968) 'Polyneuropathy in childhood.' *Acta Paediatrica Scandinavica,* **57,** 230-238.

Gath, I., Kayan, A., Leegaard, J., Sjaastad, O. (1970) 'Myasthenia congenita: electromyographic findings.' *Acta Neurologica Scandinavica,* **46,** 323-330.

Gatfield, P. D., Taller, E., Hinton, G. G., Wallace, A. C., Abdelnour, G. M., Haust, M. D. (1968) 'Hyperpipecolatemia, a new metabolic disorder associated with neuropathy and hepatomegaly: A case study.' *Canadian Medical Association Journal,* **99,** 1215.

Ghadimi, H., Binnington, V. I., Pecora, P. (1965) 'Hyperlysinemia associated with retardation.' *New England Journal of Medicine,* **272,** 723-729.

Gillberg, C. (1977) ' "Floppy infant syndrome" and maternal diazepam.' *Lancet,* **2,** 244. *(Letter.)*

Gitzelmann, R., Steinmann, B., Otten, A., Dumermuth, G., Herdan, M., Reubi, J., Cuenod, M. (1977) 'Nonketotic hyperglycinemia treated with strychnine, a glycine receptor antagonist.' *Helvetica Paediatrica Acta,* **32,** 517-525.

Goebel, H. H., Zeman, W., DeMyer, W. (1976) 'Peripheral motor and sensory neuropathy of early childhood simulating Werdnig-Hoffmann disease.' *Neuropädiatrie,* **7,** 182-195.

Gonatas, N. K., Perez, M. C., Shy, G. M., Evangelist, I. (1965) 'Central "core" disease of skeletal muscle. Ultrastructural and cytochemical observations in two cases.' *American Journal of Pathology,* **47,** 503-524.

—— Shy, G. M., Godfrey, E. H. (1966) 'Nemaline myopathy. The origin of nemaline structures.' *New England Journal of Medicine,* **274,** 535-539.

Greenfield, J. G., Stern, R. O. (1927) 'The anatomical identity of the Werdnig-Hoffmann and Oppenheim forms of infantile muscular atrophy.' *Brain,* **50,** 652-686.

—— Cornman, T., Shy, G. M. (1958) 'The prognostic value of the muscle biopsy in the floppy infant.' *Brain,* **81,** 461-484.

Haas, R. H., Robinson, A., Evans, K., Lascelles, P. T., Dubowitz, V. (1980) 'An X-linked disease of the nervous system with disordered copper metabolism and features differing from Menkes' kinky hair disease.' *(Submitted for publication).*

Habermann, J. V. (1910) 'Myatonia congenita of Oppenheim or congenital atonic pseudoparalysis.' *American Journal of the Medical Sciences,* **139,** 383-401.

Hackett, T. N., Bray, P. F., Ziter, F. A., Nyham, W. L., Creer, K. M. (1973) 'A metabolic myopathy associated with chronic lactic acidemia, growth failure, and nerve deafness.' *Journal of Pediatrics*, **83**, 426-431.

Hagberg, B., Sourander, P., Thorén, L. (1962) 'Peripheral nerve changes in the diagnosis of metachromatic leucodystrophy.' *Acta Paediatrica Scandinavica*, Suppl. **135**, 63-71.

Harper, P. S. (1975a) 'Congenital myotonic dystrophy in Britain. I. Clinical aspects.' *Archives of Disease in Childhood*, **50**, 505-513.

—— (1975b) 'Congenital myotonic dystrophy in Britain. II. Genetic basis.' *Archives of Disease in Childhood*, **50**, 514-521.

—— (1979) *Myotonic Dystrophy*. Philadelphia: W. B. Saunders.

—— Dyken, P. R. (1972) 'Early-onset dystrophia myotonica. Evidence supporting a maternal environment factor.' *Lancet*, **2**, 53-55.

—— Rivas, M. L., Bias, W. B., Hutchinson, J. R., Dyken, P. R., McKusick, V. A. (1972) 'Genetic linkage confirmed between the locus for myotonic dystrophy and the ABH-secretion and Lutheran blood group loci.' *American Journal of Human Genetics*, **24**, 310-316.

Haydar, N. A., Conn, H. L., Afifi, A., Wakid, N., Ballas, S., Fawaz, K. (1971) 'Severe hypermetabolism with primary abnormality of skeletal muscle mitochondria: functional and therapeutic effects of chloramphenicol treatment.' *Annals of Internal Medicine*, **74**, 548-558.

Heffner, R., Cohen, M., Duffner, P., Daigler, G. (1976) 'Multicore disease in twins.' *Journal of Neurology, Neurosurgery and Psychiatry*, **39**, 602-606.

Hers, H. G. (1963) 'α Glucosidase deficiency in generalised glycogen-storage disease (Pompe's disease).' *Biochemical Journal*, **86**, 11-16.

—— (1965) 'Inborn lyosomal diseases'. *Gastroenterology*, **48**, 625-633.

Hertl, M. (1977) *Pädiatrische Differentialdiagnose*. George Thieme Velag, Stuttgart, p. 532.

Hoffmann, J. (1893) 'Über chronische spinale Muskelatrophie in Kindesalter auf familiarer Basis.' *Deutsche Zeitschrift für Nervenkrankheiten*, **3**, 427-470.

—— (1897) 'Weitere Beitrage zur Lehre von der hereditären progressiven spinalen Muskelatrophie im Kindesalter.' *Deutsche Zeitschrift für Nervenkrankheiten*, **10**, 292-320.

—— (1900) 'Dritter Beitrag zur Lehre von der hereditären progressiven spinalen Muskelatrophie im Kindesalter.' *Deutsche Zeitschrift für Nervenkrankheiten*, **18**, 217-224.

Holleman, L. W. J., van der Haar, J. A., de Vaan, G. A. M. (1966) 'Type IV glycogenesis.' *Laboratory Investigation*, **15**, 357-367.

Holmes, J. B. (1920) 'Amyotonia congenita (Oppenheim).' *American Journal of Diseases of Children*, **20**, 405-435.

Holt, J. G., Hansen, A. E. (1951) 'Management of newborn infant with symptoms indicative of myasthenia gravis.' *Texas State Journal of Medicine*, **47**, 299-302.

Hommes, F. A. Kuipers, J. R. G., Elema, J. D., Jansen, J. F. Jonxis, J. J. P. (1968) 'Propionicacidemia: a new inborn error of metabolism.' *Pediatric Research*, **2**, 519-524.

Hopkins, I. J., Lindsey, J. R., Ford, F. R. (1966) 'Nemaline myopathy. A long-term clinico-pathologic study of affected mother and daughter.' *Brain*, **89**, 299-310.

Hudgson, P., Gardner-Medwin, D., Fulthorpe, J. J., Walton, J. N. (1967) 'Nemaline myopathy.' *Neurology*, **17**, 1125-1142.

Huenekens, E. J., Bell, E. T. (1920) 'Infantile spinal progressive muscular atrophy (Werdnig-Hoffmann).' *American Journal of Diseases of Children*, **20**, 496-506.

Hutchison, A. A., Lloyd, D. J., Russell, G. (1975) 'Monitoring muscle weakness in neonatal myasthenia gravis.' *British Medical Journal*, **4**, 623-624.

Huttenlocher, P. R., Gilles, F. H. (1967) 'Infantile neuraxonal dystrophy.' *Neurology*, **17**, 1174-1184.

Jatzkewitz, H. (1966) 'Evidence for metabolic blocks in sphingolipidoses.' *In:* Luthy, F., Bischoff, A. (Eds.) *Proceedings of the 5th International Congress of Neuropathology, Sept. 1965, Zurich. I.C.S. No. 100.* Amsterdam: Excerpta Medica. pp. 417-421.

Jebsen, R. H., Johnson, E. W., Knobloch, H., Grant, D. K. (1961) 'Differential diagnosis of infantile hypotonia: the use of the electromyograph and the developmental and neurologic examination as aids.' *American Journal of Diseases of Children*, **101**, 8-17.

Jerusalem, F., Engel, A. G., Gomez, M. R. (1973a) 'Sarcotubular myopathy: a newly recognized, benign, congenital, familial muscle disease.' *Neurology*, **23**, 897-906.

—— Angelini, C., Engel, A. G., Groover, R. V. (1973b) 'Mitochondrial-lipid-glycogen (MLG) disease of muscle.' *Archives of Neurology*, **29**, 162-169.

Jeffcoate, W. J., Laurance, B. M., Edwards, C. R. W., Besser, G. M. (1980) 'Endocrine function in the Prader-Willi syndrome.' *Clinical Endocrinology*, **12**, 81-89.

Jervis, G. A., (1950) 'Early familial cerebellar degeneration (report of three cases in one family).' *Journal of Nervous and Mental Disease*, **111**, 398-407.

Jones, R., Khan, R., Hughes, S., Dubowitz, V. (1979) 'Congenital muscular dystrophy: the importance of early diagnosis and orthopaedic management in the long term prognosis.' *Journal of Bone and Joint Surgery*, **61B**, 13-17.

Karpati, G., Carpenter, S., Nelson, R. F. (1970) 'Type I muscle fibre atrophy and central nuclei. A rare familial neuromuscular disease.' *Journal of the Neurological Sciences*, **10**, 489-500.

150

———— Andermann, F. (1971) 'A new concept of childhood nemaline myopathy.' *Archives of Neurology.* **24**, 291-304.
———— Engel, A. G., Watters, G., Allen, J., Rothman, S., Klassen, G., Mamer, O. A. (1975) 'The syndrome of systemic carnitine deficiency.' *Neurology.* **25**, 16-24.
Kasman, M., Bernstein, L., Schulman, S. (1976) 'Chronic polyradiculoneuropathy of infancy: a report of three cases with familial incidence.' *Neurology.* **26**, 565-573.
Kearns, T. P., Sayre, G. P. (1958) 'Retinitis pigmentosa, external ophthalmoplegia and complete heart block.' *Archives of Ophthalmology (Chicago).* **60**, 280-289.
Keeton, B. R., Moosa, A. (1976) 'Organic aciduria: treatable cause of floppy infant syndrome.' *Archives of Disease in Childhood.* **51**, 636-638.
Key, J. A. (1927) 'Hypermobility of joints as a sex-linked hereditary characteristic.' *Journal of the American Medical Association.* **88**, 1710-1712.
Kinoshita, M., Cadman, T. E. (1968) 'Myotubular myopathy.' *Archives of Neurology.* **18**, 265-271.
Kott, E., Bornstein, B. (1969) 'Familial early infantile myasthenia gravis with a 15-year follow-up.' *Journal of the Neurological Sciences.* **8**, 573-578.
Krabbe, K. H. (1947) 'Kongenit generaliseret muskelaplasi.' *Nordisk Medicin.* **35**, 1756.
—— (1958) 'Congenital generalised muscular atrophies.' *Acta Psychiatrica et Neurologica.* **33**, 94-102.
Kucerová, M., Strakova, M., Polívková, Z. (1979) 'The Prader-Willi syndrome with a 15/3 translocation.' *Journal of Medical Genetics.* **16**, 234-235.
Kuitonnen, P., Rapola, J., Noponen, A. L., Donner, M. (1972) 'Nemaline myopathy. Report of 4 cases and review of literature.' *Acta Paediatrica Scandinavica.* **61**, 353-361.
Lake, B. D., Wilson, J. (1975) 'Zebra body myopathy: clinical, histochemical and ultrastructural studies.' *Journal of the Neurological Sciences.* **24**, 437-446.
Lebenthal, E., Schochet, S. R., Adam, A., Seelenfreund, M., Fried, A., Najenson, T., Sandbank, U., Matoth, Y. (1970) 'Arthrogryposis multiplex congenita—23 cases in an Arab kindred.' *Pediatrics.* **46**, 891-899.
Lenard, H. G., Goebel, H. H. (1975) 'Congenital fibre type disproportion.' *Neuropädiatrie.* **6**, 220-231.
—— —— Weigel, W. (1977) 'Smooth muscle involvement in congenital myotonic dystrophy.' *Neuropädiatrie.* **8**, 48-52.
Lesný, I. A. (1979) 'Follow-up study of hypotonic forms of cerebral palsy.' *Brain and Development.* **1**, 87-90.
Levin, P. M. (1949) 'Congenital myasthenia gravis in siblings.' *Archives of Neurology and Psychiatry.* **62**, 745-758.
Lowe, C. U., Terry, M., MacLachlan, E. A. (1952) 'Organicaciduria, decreased renal ammonia production, hydrophthalmos, and mental retardation: a clinical entity.' *American Journal of Diseases of Children.* **83**, 164-184.
Luft, R., Ikkos, D., Palmieri, G., Ernster, L., Afzelius, B. (1962) 'A case of severe hypermetabolism of nonthyroid origin with a defect in the maintenance of mitochondrial respiratory control. A correlated clinical, biochemical and morphological study.' *Journal of Clinical Investigation.* **41**, 1776-1804.
Mabry, C. C., Karam, E. A. (1963) 'Idiopathic hyperglycinemia and hyperglycinuria.' *Southern Medical Journal.* **56**, 1444. *(Summary).*
Matsumoto, T., Mitsudome, A., Nagayama, T. (1970) 'Progressive muscular dystrophy in infancy.' *Acta Paediatrica Japonica.* **12**, 4-8.
McKusick, V. A. (1972) *Heritable Disorders of Connective Tissue. 4th Edition.* St. Louis: C. V. Mosby.
—— (1976) 'Heritable disorders of connective tissue: new clinical and biochemical aspects.' *In:* Turner, P. (Ed.) *Advanced Medicine. Vol. 12. 1976.* London: Pitman Medical, pp. 170-191.
——Neufeld, E. F., Kelly, T. E. (1978) 'The mucopolysaccharide storage diseases.' *In* Stanbury, J. B., Wyngaarden, J. B., Fredrickson, D. S. (Eds.) *The Metabolic Basis of Inherited Disease, 4th Edition.* Maidenhead: McGraw-Hill, pp. 1282-1307.
—— Kaplan, D., Wise, D., Hanley, E. B., Suddarth, S. B., Sevick, M. E., Maunanee, A. E. (1965) 'The genetic mucopolysaccharidoses.' *Medicine.* **44**, 445-483.
McLean, W. T., McKone, R. C. (1973) 'Congenital myasthenia gravis in twins.' *Archives of Neurology.* **29**, 223-226.
Macrae, D. (1954) 'Myasthenia gravis in early childhood.' *Pediatrics.* **13**, 511-520.
Menkes, J. H. (1980) *Textbook of Child Neurology. 2nd Edition.* Philadelphia: Lea & Febiger.
Millichap, J. G., Dodge, P. R. (1960) 'Diagnosis and treatment of myasthenia gravis in infancy, childhood and adolescence. A study of 51 patients.' *Neurology.* **10**, 1007-1014.
Mohr, J. (1954) *A Study of Linkage in Man. Vol 33. Opera ex domo biologiae hereditariae humanae universitatis hafniensis.* Copenhagen: Munksgaard.
Moosa, A. (1974) 'The feeding difficulty in infantile myotonic dystrophy.' *Developmental Medicine and Child Neurology.* **16**, 824-825.
—— (1975) 'Peripheral neuropathy in Leigh's encephalomyelopathy.' *Developmental Medicine and Child Neurology.* **17**, 621-640.
—— Dubowitz, V. (1970) 'Peripheral neuropathy in Cockayne's syndrome.' *Archives of Disease in Childhood.* **45**, 674-677.
—— —— (1971) 'Slow nerve conduction velocity in cretins.' *Archives of Disease in Childhood.* **46**, 852-854.

151

—— —— (1973) 'Spinal muscular atrophy in childhood: two clues to clinical diagnosis.' *Archives of Disease in Childhood.* **48**, 386-388.

—— —— —— (1976) 'Motor nerve conduction velocity in spinal muscular atrophy of childhood.' *Archives of Disease in Childhood.* **51**, 974-977.

Mouton, C. M., Smillie, J. G., Bower, A. G. (1950) 'Report of ten cases of poliomyelitis in infants under 6 months of age.' *Journal of Pediatrics.* **36**, 482-492.

Munsat, T. L., Thompson, L. R., Coleman, R. F. (1969) 'Centronuclear ('Myotubular') myopathy.' *Archives of Neurology.* **20**, 120-131.

Namba, T., Brunner, N. G., Brown, S. B., Mugurama, M., Grob, D. (1971a) 'Familial myasthenia gravis.' *Archives of Neurology.* **25**, 61-72.

—— Shapiro, M. S., Brunner, N. G., Grob, D. (1971b) 'Myasthenia gravis occurring in twins.' *Journal of Neurology. Neurosurgery and Psychiatry.* **34**, 531-534.

Nausieda, P. A., Klawans, H. L. (1977) 'Lipid storage disorders.' *In:* Vinken, P. J., Bruyn, G. W. (Eds.) *Handbook of Clinical Neurology. Vol. 29: Metabolic and Deficiency Diseases of the Nervous System. Part III:* Amsterdam: North-Holland, p. 350.

Neville, H. E., Brooke, M. H. (1973) 'Central core fibres: structured and unstructured.' *In:* Kakulas, B. A. (Ed.) *Basic Research in Myology. Proceedings of 2nd International Congress on Muscle Diseases. Perth, Australia, November 1971. Part 1, I.C.S. No. 294.* Amsterdam: Excerpta Medica, pp. 497-511.

Nonaka, I., Miyoshino, S., Miike, T., Ueno, T., Usuku, G. (1972) 'An electron microscopical study of the muscle in congenital muscular dystrophy. '*Kumamoto Medical Journal.* **25**, 68-82.

Oberholzer, V. G., Levin, B., Burgess, E. A., Young, W. F. (1967) 'Methylmalonic aciduria. An inborn error of metabolism leading to chronic metabolic acidosis.' *Archives of Disease in Childhood.* **42**, 492-504.

Oberklaid, F., Hopkins, I. J. (1976) '"Juvenile" myasthenia gravis in early infancy.' *Archives of Disease in Childhood.* **51**, 719-721.

Olson, W., Engel, W. K., Walsh, G. O., Einaugler, R. (1972) 'Oculocraniosomatic neuromuscular disease with "ragged-red" fibers.' *Archives of Neurology.* **26**, 193-211.

Oppenheim, H. (1900) 'Ueber allgemeine und localisierte Atonie der Muskulatur (Myatonie) im frühen Kindesalter.' *Monatsschrift für Psychiatrie und Neurologie.* **8**, 232-233.

—— (1904) 'Ueber einen Fall von Myotonia congenita.' *Berliner klinische Wochenschrift.* **41**, 255.

—— (1912) 'Fall von Myotonia congenita. Demonstration in Hufelandische Geselschaft. No. 14, 1912.' *Berliner klinische Wochenschrift.* **49**, 2435.

Ortiz de Zarate, J. C., Maruffo, A. (1970) 'The descending ocular myopathy of early childhood. Myotubular or centronuclear myopathy.' *European Neurology.* **3**, 1-12.

Osserman, K. E. (1958) *Myasthenia Gravis.* New York: Grune & Stratton.

Paine, R. S. (1963) 'The future of the "floppy infant": a follow-up study of 133 patients.' *Developmental Medicine and Child Neurology.* **5**, 115-124.

—— Oppé, T. E. (1966) *Neurological Examination of Children. Clinics in Developmental Medicine Nos. 20/21.* London: S.I.M.P. with Heinemann Medical; Philadelphia: Lippincott.

Papatestas, A. E., Genkins, G., Kark, A. E. (1973) 'Thymectomy for myasthenia gravis.' *British Medical Journal.* **2**, 306. (Letter.)

Pearn, J. H., Carter, C. O., Wilson, J. (1973) 'The genetic identity of acute infantile spinal muscular atrophy.' *Brain.* **96**, 463-470.

Perheentupa, J., Autio, S., Leisti, A., Raitta, C., Tuuteri, L. (1973) 'Mulibrey nanism, an autosomal recessive syndrome with pericardial constriction.' *Lancet.* **2**, 351-355.

—— —— —— —— —— (1975) 'Mulibrey nanism: review of 23 cases of a new autosomal recessive syndrome.' *Birth Defects. Original Article Series XI.* (2), 3-17.

Peterman, A. F., Daly, D. D., Dion, F. R., Keith, H. M. (1959) 'Infectious neuronitis (Guillain-Barré syndrome) in children.' *Neurology.* **9**, 533-539.

Pickett, J., Berg, B., Chaplin, E., Brunstetter-Shafer, M. (1976) 'Syndrome of botulism in infancy: clinical and electrophysiologic study.' *New England Journal of Medicine.* **295**, 769-772.

Pope, F. M., Nicholls, A. C. (1978) 'Molecular abnormalities of collagen.' *Journal of Clinical Pathology.* **30**, Suppl. 12, 95-104.

Prader, A., Labhardt, A., Willi, H. (1956) 'Ein Syndrom von Adipositas, Kleinwuchs, Kryptorchismus und Oligophrenie nach myotonieartigem Zustand im Neugeborenenalter.' *Schweizerische medizinische Wochenschrift.* **86**, 1260-1261.

—— Willi, H. (1963) 'Das Syndrom von Imbezillitat, Adipositas, Muskelhypotonie, hypogonadismus und Diabetes Mellitus mit "Myotonie-" Anamnese.' in: *Verhand 2nd International Kongress der Psychiatrie und Entwicklungs-Storungen die Kindesalter, Vienna, 1961. Part 1.* p. 353-357.

Prechtl, H. F. R., Beintema, D. (1964) *The Neurological Examination of the Full Term Newborn Infant. Clinics in Developmental Medicine No. 12.* London: S.I.M.P. with Heinemann Medical; Philadelphia: Lippincott.

Price, H. M., Gordon, G. B., Pearson, C. M., Munsat, T. L., Blumberg, J. M. (1965) 'New evidence for excessive accumulation of Z-band material in nemaline myopathy.' *Proceedings of the National Academy of Sciences of the U.S.A. (Washington).* **54**, 1398-1406.

Rabe, E. F. (1964) 'The hypotonic infant.' *Journal of Pediatrics.* **64**, 422-440.

Ramsey, P. L., Hensinger, R. N. (1975) 'Congenital dislocation of the hip associated with central core disease.' *Journal of Bone and Joint Surgery,* **57A,** 648-651.

Reed, G. B., Dixon, J. F. P., Neustein, H. B., Donnell, G. N., Landing, B. H. (1968) 'Type IV glycogenosis. Patient with absence of a branching enzyme α-1,4-glucan:α-1,4-glucan 6-glycosyl transferase.' *Laboratory Investigation,* **19,** 546-557.

Renwick, J. H., Bundey, S. E., Ferguson-Smith, M. A., Izatt, M. M. (1971) 'Confirmation of linkage of the loci for myotonic dystrophy and ABH secretion.' *Journal of Medical Genetics,* **8,** 407-416.

Richards, W., Donnell, G. N., Wilson, W. A., Stowens, D., Perry, T. (1965) 'The oculo-cerebro-renal syndrome of Lowe.' *American Journal of Diseases of Children,* **109,** 185-203.

Rothmann, M. (1909) 'Ueber die anatomische Grundlage der Myotonia congenita.' *Monatsschrift für Psychiatrie und Neurologie,* **25,** 161-185.

Rotthauwe, H. W., Kowalewski, S., Mumenthaler, M. (1969) 'Kongenitale Muskeldystrophie.' *Zeitschrift für Kinderheilkunde,* **106,** 131-162.

Sandifer, P. H. (1955) 'The differential diagnosis of flaccid paralysis.' *Proceedings of the Royal Society of Medicine,* **48,** 186-189.

Santavuori, P., Haltia, M., Rapola, J. (1974) 'Infantile type of so-called neuronal ceroid-lipofuscinosis.' *Developmental Medicine and Child Neurology,* **16,** 644-653.

—— Leisti, J., Kruus, S. (1977) 'Muscle, eye and brain disease: a new syndrome.' *Neuropädiatrie,* **8,** (Suppl.), 553.

Schochet, S. S., McCormick, W. F., Zellweger, H. (1970) 'Type IV glycogenosis (amylopectinosis): light and electron microscopic observations.' *Archives of Pathology,* **90,** 354-363.

Segawa, M. (1970) 'Clinical studies of congenital muscular dystrophy. Arthrogrypotic type congenital muscular dystrophy with mental retardation and facial muscle involvement.' *Brain and Development,* **2,** 439-451.

—— Fukuyama, Y., Itoh, K., Uono, M. (1970) 'Congenital muscular dystrophy (with progressive development of joint contracture, mental retardation and facial involvement). I. Clinical studies.' *Brain and Development (Tokyo),* **2,** 67.

Seitelberger, F. (1952) 'Eine unbekannte Form von infantiler lipoidspeicher Krankheit des Gehirns.' *Proceedings of First International Congress of Neuropathology, Rome, Vol. 3.* Turin: Rosenberg and Sellier, p. 323.

—— Wanko, T., Gavin, M. A. (1961) 'The muscle fibre in central core disease. Histochemical and electron microscopic observations.' *Acta Neuropathologica,* **1,** 223-237.

Sengers, R. C. A., ter Haar, B. G., Trijbels, J. M. F., Willems, J. L., Daniels, O., Stadhouders, A. M. (1975) 'Congenital cataract and mitochondrial myopathy of skeletal and heart muscle associated with lactic acidosis after exercise.' *Journal of Pediatrics,* **86,** 873-880.

Shafiq, S. A., Dubowitz, V., Peterson, H. de C., Milhorat, A. T. (1967) 'Nemaline myopathy. Report of a fatal case with histochemical and electron microscopic studies.' *Brain,* **90,** 817-828.

Shelokov, A., Weinstein, L. (1951) 'Poliomyelitis in the early neonatal period: report of a case with possible intrauterine infection.' *Journal of Pediatrics,* **38,** 80-84.

Sher, J. H., Rimalovski, A. B., Athanassiades, T. J., Arowson, S. M. (1967) 'Familial myotubular myopathy: a clinical, pathological, histochemical and ultrastructural study.' *Journal of Neuropathology and Experimental Neurology,* **26,** 132-133.

Shy, G. M., Engel, W. K., Somers, J. E., Wanko, T. (1963) 'Nemaline myopathy—a new congenital myopathy.' *Brain,* **86,** 793-810.

—— Magee, K. R. (1956) 'A new congenital non-progressive myopathy.' *Brain,* **79,** 610-621.

—— Gonatas, N. K., Perez, M. (1966) 'Two childhood myopathies with abnormal mitochondria. I. Megaconial myopathy. II. Pleoconial myopathy.' *Brain,* **89,** 133-158.

Sinclair, L. (1979) *Metabolic Disease in Childhood.* Oxford: Blackwell.

Smyth, D. P. L., Lake, B. D., MacDermot, J., Wilson, J. (1975) 'Inborn error of carnitine metabolism ('carnitine deficiency') in man.' *Lancet,* **1,** 1198-1199, *(Letter.)*

Sobel, J. (1926) 'Essential or primary hypotonia in young children.' *Medical Journal and Record,* **124,** 225-230.

Sourander, P., Olsson, Y. (1968) 'Peripheral neuropathy in globoid cell leucodystrophy.' *Acta Neuropathologica,* **11,** 69-81.

Spiro, A. J., Kennedy, C. (1965) 'Hereditary occurrence of nemaline myopathy.' *Archives of Neurology,* **13,** 155-159.

—— Shy, G. M., Gonatas, N. K. (1966) 'Myotubular myopathy.' *Archives of Neurology,* **14,** 1-14.

Stokke, O., Jellum, E., Eldjarn, L. (1972) 'A new metabolic error in the leucine degradation pathway: β-hydroxyisovaleric aciduria and β-methylcrotonyl glycinuria.' *In:* Stern, J., Toothill, C. (Eds.) *Organic Acidurias.* Edinburgh: Churchill & Livingstone, pp. 27-34.

Sturkie, P. D. (1941) 'Hypermobile joints in all descendents for two generations.' *Journal of Heredity,* **32,** 232-234.

Sutro, C. J. (1947) 'Hypermobility of bones due to "over lengthened" capsular and ligamentous tissues; cause for recurrent intra-articular effusions.' *Surgery,* **21,** 67-76.

Svennerholm, L., Hagberg, B., Haltia, M., Sourander, P., Vanier, M-T. (1975) 'Polyunsaturated fatty acid lipidosis (PFAL). II: Lipid biochemical studies.' *Acta Paediatrica Scandinavica,* **64,** 489-496.

Teng, P., Osserman, K. E. (1956) 'Studies in myasthenia gravis: neonatal and juvenile types.' *Journal of the Mount Sinai Hospital,* **23,** 711-727.

Tizard, J. P. M. (1954) 'General comments on examination and clinical signs.' *In:* Gaisford, W., Lightwood, R. (Eds.) *Paediatrics for the Practitioner.* London: Butterworth, pp. 3-26.

Tomé, F. M. S., Fardeau, M. (1976) 'Ultrastructural study of a muscle biopsy in a case of G_{M1} gangliosidosis type 1.' *Pathologia Europaea,* **11,** 15-25.

Trijbels, J. M. F., Monnens, L. A. H., Bakkeren, J. A. J. M., Van Raay-Selten, A. J. H., Corstiaensen, J. M. B. (1979) 'Biochemical studies in the cerebro-hepato-renal syndrome of Zellweger: a disturbance in the metabolism of pipecolic acid.' *Journal of Inherited Metabolic Disease,* **2,** 39-42.

Turner, H. D., Brett, E. M., Gilbert, R. J., Ghosh, A. C., Liebeschuetz, H. J. (1978) 'Infant botulism in England.' *Lancet,* **1,** 1277-1278.

Turner, J. W. A. (1940) 'The relationship between amyotonia congenita and congenital myopathy.' *Brain,* **63,** 163-177.

Turner, J. W. A. (1949) 'On amyotonia congenita.' *Brain,* **72,** 25-34.

—— Lees, F. (1962) 'Congenital myopathy: a 50-year follow-up.' *Brain,* **85,** 733-740.

Tyrell, D. A., Ryman, B. E. E., Keeton, B. R., Dubowitz, V. (1976) 'Use of liposomes in treating type II glycogenesis.' *British Medical Journal,* **3,** 88.

Ugarte, M., Lopez-Lahoya, J., Garcia, M. L., Benavides, J., Valdivieso, F. (1980) 'Possible explanation for hyperglycinaemia in propionic acidaemia and methylmalonic acidaemia: propionate and methylmalonate inhibit liver and brain mitochondrial glycine transport.' *Journal of Inherited Metabolic Disease,* **2,** 93-96.

Vanasse, M., Dubowitz, V. (1980) 'Dominantly inherited peroneal muscular atrophy (hereditary motor and sensory neuropathy type 1) in infancy and childhood.' *(Muscle and Nerve, in press).*

VanDyke, D. H., Griggs, R. C., Markesbery, W., Di Mauro, S. (1975) 'Hereditary carnitine deficiency of muscle.' *Neurology,* **25,** 154-159.

Vanier, T. M. (1960) 'Dystrophia myotonica in childhood.' *British Medical Journal,* **2,** 1284-1288.

Vassella, F., Mumenthaler, M., Rossi, E., Moser, H., Weissman, U. (1967) 'Die kongenitale Muskeldystrophie.' *Deutsche Zeitschrift für Nervenheilkunde,* **190,** 349-374.

van Wijngaarden, G. K., Fleury, P., Bethlem, J., Meijer, A. E. F. H. (1969) 'Familial "myotubular" myopathy.' *Neurology,* **19,** 901-908.

Vital, C., Vallat, J. M., Martin, F., Le Blanc, M., Bergouignan, M. (1970) 'Étude clinique et ultra-structurale d'un cas de myopathie centronucléaire (myotubular myopathy) de l'adulte.' *Revue Neurologique,* **123,** 117-130.

Von Wendt, L., Similä, S., Hirvasniemi, A., Suvanto, E. (1978) 'Non-ketotic hyperglycinemia: a clinical analysis of 19 Finnish patients.' *Monographs in Human Heredity,* **9,** 58-74.

Walton, J. N. (1956) 'Amyotonia congenita: a follow-up study.' *Lancet,* **1,** 1023-1027.

—— (1957a) 'The limp child.' *Journal of Neurology, Neurosurgery and Psychiatry,* **20,** 144-154.

—— (1957b) 'The amyotonia congenita syndrome.' *Proceedings of the Royal Society of Medicine,* **50,** 301-308.

Werdnig, G. (1891) 'Zwei frühinfantile hereditäre Fälle von progressiver Muskelatrophie unter dem Bilde der Dystrophie, aber auf neurotischer Grundlage.' *Archiv für Psychiatrie und Nervenkrankheiten,* **22,** 437-481.

—— (1894) 'Die frühinfantile progressive spinale Amyotrophie.' *Archiv für Psychiatrie und Nervenkrankheiten,* **26,** 706-744.

Woody, N. C. (1964) 'Hyperlysinemia.' *American Journal of Diseases of Children,* **108,** 543-553.

—— Hutzler, J., Dancis, J. (1966) 'Further studies of hyperlysinemia.' *American Journal of Diseases of Children,* **112,** 577-580.

Yannet, H., Horton, F. H. (1952) 'Hypotonic cerebral palsy in mental defectives.' *Pediatrics,* **9,** 204-211.

Zellweger, H. (1946) 'Ueber verschiedene Formen von Muskelhypotonie im Kindesalter.' *Helvetica Paediatrica Acta,* **1,** 427-448.

—— Smith, J. W., Cusminsky, M. (1962) 'Muscular hypotonia in infancy: diagnosis and differentiation.' *Revue Canadienne de Biologie,* **21,** 599-612.

—— Afifi, A., McCormick, W. F., Mergner, W. (1967a) 'Benign congenital muscular dystrophy: a special form of congenital hypotonia.' *Clinical Pediatrics,* **6,** 655-663.

—— —— —— —— (1967b) 'Severe congenital muscular dystrophy.' *American Journal of Diseases of Children,* **114,** 591-602.

INDEX

Note: Main treatment of a subject is indicated by figures in **bold type**. Illustrations are indicated *in italics* only when they occur on a different page from the corresponding text.

A

Acetylcholine receptor antibody, in neonatal myasthenia 87
Amino acid metabolic disorders 105
Amniocentesis, for congenital myotonic dystrophy 77
Amyotonia congenita 3
  causes 4 *(tables)*
Arachidonic acid metabolic error 109
Arthrochalasis multiplex congenita 116
Arthrogryposis, 77, 82, 140

B

Benign congenital (essential) hypotonia 133-138
Biotin therapy 108
Birth trauma 100
  sucking/swallowing difficulty 140
Botulism 89

C

Cardiomyopathy, in congenital myotonic dystrophy 75
Carnitine deficiency 69
  palmityl transferase 70
Central core disease 6, **35**
  coexistence with nemaline myopathy 47
Central nervous system, causative role 14, *15*
  disorders 96-114
    progressive degenerative 92
Centronuclear myopathy. *See* Myotubular myopathy
Ceramide 111
Cerebral haemorrhage, neonatal 100
Cerebral palsy, hypotonic 99
Cerebro-hepato-renal syndrome 111
Charcot-Marie-Tooth disease 91
Chromosomal disorders 103
Clinical examination 10-18
Clinical features, role in differential diagnosis 139
Cockayne's syndrome 94
Coeliac disease 132
Collagen disorders 115
Congenital disorders
  dislocation of the hip 36, 117
  fibre type disproportion 50
    type 1 54
  heart disease 133, *134*
  laxity of ligaments 115, *118*
  muscular dystrophy 77-86
    clinical picture 82
    genetics 85
    investigations 84
    management 85

myopathy 5, 33-71
  clinical features 33
  investigations 34
  non-specific 61
  structural 35-62
myotonic dystrophy 72-77
  intra-uterine causalogy 75
  sucking/swallowing difficulty 139
Connective tissue disorders 17, 115-125
  classification 124 *(table)* 125 *(table)*
  heritable 115, 123 *(table)*
Copper metabolism anomalies 105
Creatine phosphokinase, serum
  congenital myopathy 34
  in diagnosis 143
  spinal muscular atrophy of intermediate severity 30
Cytochrome oxidase deficiency 56

D

Deformity, prevention of, in spinal muscular atrophy of intermediate severity 30
Diabetes, of Prader-Willi syndrome 126
Diagnostic procedures 139-145
Diaphragmatic hypoplasia 72
Diazepam, perinatal influence 100
Dejerine-Sottas peripheral neuropathy 91
Down's syndrome 103, *104*, 133
Drugs, perinatal influences 100
Duchenne muscular dystrophy 86, 144

E

Edrophonium therapy 89
Ehler-Danlos syndrome 116, *119*, *120*
  classification 115, 124 *(table)*
Electrodiagnosis 141
Electronmicroscopy 144
Electromyography 142
Endocrine disorders 133, *134*
Enzymes
  deficiency, in progressive degenerative disorders of the CNS 92
  histochemistry, role in muscle biopsy 144
  lipid storage disorders 112 *(table)*
  serum, in diagnosis 143
Essential (benign congenital) hypotonia 6, 133-138

F

Facial weakness 140
Facies, in congenital myotonic dystrophy 72, *76*, 140

155

Mulibrey nanism 110
  Prader-Willi syndrome 126, *127*
Familial dysautonomia 94
Fingerprint myopathy 61
Flexor muscle resistance, in assessment 11
Floppy infant syndrome. *See* Hypotonia
Frog posture 10, *21*
Fukuyama syndrome 81, 85

G

Galactosyl-ceramide *β*-galactosidase, deficiency 92
Gangliosidases 94, 111, *112*
Gestational age, factor in assessment 11
Globoid cell leucodystrophy 92
Globosides 111
Glycine encephalopathy 107
Glycogen storage myopathy 56
Glycogenoses 63, 64 *(table)*
  Type II (Pompe's disease) 63-67, 133
  Type III 67
  Type IV 69
Guillain-Barré syndrome 91

H

Hands, passive movements, in congenital muscular dystrophy 86
Heart disease, congenital 67, 133, *134*
Hereditary motor and sensory neuropathy (HMSN) 91
HMSN (hereditary motor and sensory neuropathy) 91
Honey, contamination with Cl. botulinum 89
Hunter's syndrome 105
Hydramnios 72
β-Hydroxyisovaleric acidaemia 108
5-Hydroxytryptophan, therapeutic 103
Hyperglycinaemia, non-ketotic 106
Hyperlysinaemia 105
Hypertrophic neuropathy 91
Hypertrophy, type 1, with central nuclei 43
Hypothyroidism, infantile 133, *134*
Hypotonia
  assessment 10
  benign congenital (essential) 5, 6, **133-139**
  causes, anatomical approach *14*
  classification 11
    Jebsen 7 *(table)*
    Walton 6 *(table)*
    Zellweger 8 *(table)*
  clinical features 1
  differential diagnosis 11
  essential (benign congenital) 5, 6, **133-138**
  historical aspects 1-9
  isolated 17
  neuromuscular causes (Rabe) 9 *(table)*
  nomenclature, historical background 2-9
  symptomatic 5
  without significant weakness 95
Hypotonia-obesity (Prader-Willi) syndrome 7, **126-131**
Hypotonic cerebral palsy 99
Hypoxia, neonatal 100

I

Inborn errors of metabolism 105-111
Infantile progressive spinal muscular atrophy 2
Infectious polyneuropathy 91

K

Kearns-Sayre's syndrome 56
Kinky hair syndrome 56, 105
Krabbe's disease 92
Kugelberg-Welander syndrome 26
Kyphoscoliosis 72

L

Lactate, metabolic disorder 107
Laxity of ligaments, congenital 115, 117, *118*, *119*
Leigh's syndrome (encephalomyelopathy) 56, 94, 107
Lesch-Nyhan's syndrome 105
Leucodystrophy, demyelinating 92
  peripheral neuropathy 113
Lipid metabolism, abnormalities 69
Lipid storage myopathy 56
  enzyme defects 112 *(table)*
Liposome replacement therapy 67
Liver enlargement, in glycogenosis 67
Lowe's syndrome (oculo-cerebro-renal syndrome) 105, 111

M

Marfan syndrome 116, *121*, 124 *(table)*, 133
Menkes syndrome 56, 105
Mental retardation 17
  central nervous system disorders 96
  congenital myotonic dystrophy 75
  hypotonic cerebral palsy 99
  non-specific 96
Metabolic disorders 105-111
  hypotonia 132
  myopathy 63-71
Metachromatic leucodystrophy 92
β-Methylcrotonyl coenzyme A deficiency 108
Methylmalonic acidaemia 107
Minicore disease 38, 48
Minimal change myopathy 51, **61**
Mitochondrial myopathy 7, 33, **54**
Mitochondrial-lipid-glycogen storage myopathy 56
Mixed myopathy 47
Mongolism 103, *104*, 133
Morquio-Brailsford syndrome 117, *122*
Motor cranial nerves, in Werdnig-Hoffmann disease 25
Mucopolysaccharidoses 117, *122*, 125 *(table)*
Mucopolysaccharidoses II: 105
Mulibrey nanism 110
Muscle, eye and brain disease 110
Muscle biopsy **144**
  central core disease 36
  congenital fibre type disproportion 50
  congenital muscular dystrophy 84
  sphingolipidoses 114

spinal muscular atrophy of intermediate severity 26-32
Type II glycogenosis 67
Type III glycogenosis 69
Werdnig-Hoffmann disease 23, *25*
Myasthenia
congenital (infantile) 88
electromyography 143
neonatal 87
sucking/swallowing difficulty 140
Myotonia congenita 3, 143
Myotubular myopathy 6, 41
severe X-linked 44
with type 1 fibre hypotrophy 43

N

Nemaline myopathy 6, **38**, 47
Neostigmine therapy 87, 89
Nerve conduction velocity 141
sensory 141
Neuroaxonal dystrophy 92
Neuronal ceroid lipofuscinosis, infantile 109
Non-paralytic conditions 16 *(table)*
Non-progressive congenital myopathies 6
Nutritional disorders 132

O

Obesity. *See* Prader-Willi syndrome
Oculo-cerebro-renal disease (Lowe's syndrome) 105, 111
Oculocraniosomatic syndrome 55
Ophthalmoplegia, external 140
of congenital myasthenia 88
'plus' 55, 140
Organic acid disorders 107
Oxidative anomalies 47, 56

P

Paralytic conditions 16 *(table)*
and non-paralytic, differentiation 13
Patent ductus arteriosus, of congenital muscular dystrophy 82
Peptidase deficiency 116
Periodic paralysis 71
Peripheral neuropathy
acquired 89
classification, of Dyck 91
hereditary 91
lipidoses 113
Peroneal muscular atrophy 91
Phenylketonuria 105
Pipecolic acid 111
Poliomyelitis 89
Polyneuropathy 90
Pompe's disease 63-67, 133
Potassium, role in periodic paralysis 71
Prader-Willi syndrome 7, **126-131**, 140
Prednisone, treatment of carnitine deficiency 70
Propionic acidaemia 107, *108*
Pseudomyotonic bursts, in Type II glycogenosis 67
Ptosis, of congenital myasthenia 88
Pyruvate, metabolic disorder 107

R

Ragged-red fibres 55
Reducing body myopathy 60
Refsum's disease 91
Respiratory features 22, 23, 72
Rickets 132
Rod body myopathy. *See* Nemaline myopathy
Roussy-Lévy disease 91

S

Salbutamol inhalation 71
Santavuori syndrome 82
Sarcotubular myopathy 61
Scoliosis, of spinal muscular atrophy of intermediate severity 29, 30
Serum enzymes, in diagnosis 143
Smooth muscle involvement, in congenital myotonic dystrophy 75
Sphingolipidoses 111
Spinal muscular atrophy 7, **20-32**
benign variants 26
infantile. *See* Werdnig-Hoffmann's disease
intermediate severity 26-32
sucking/swallowing difficulty 140
Stains, routine 145 *(table)*
Storage disease myopathy 56
Strychnine, therapeutic 107
Succinate, metabolic disorder 107
Sucking/swallowing difficulty, role in diagnosis 139
Sulphatide lipidosis 92
Sural nerve biopsy 113

T

Talipes 72
Tay-Sachs disease *113*
Tenotomy, for congenital muscular dystrophy 85
Thomsen's disease 3
Traction on hands in supine position 11
Trauma, birth 100
Trichopoliodystrophy 56
Trisomy 21: 103, *104*

U

Universal muscular atrophy 39

V

Ventral suspension position 11
Vitamin B_{12}, treatment of methylmalonic acidaemia 107

W

Werdnig-Hoffmann's disease 2
clinical features 20
contractures 22
course and prognosis 23
diagnosis 23
genetics 26
infantile peripheral neuropathy mimicking 91

management 25
onset 20
Whorled fibres, coexistence with minicore disease
  48

Z

Zebra body myopathy 61
Zellweger's disease 111